Classic Fine Art Nudes Volume One

By

Carl Scott Harker

Copyright Notice

Cover design by Carl Scott Harker
Copyright © 2019 Carl Scott Harker

An Aldouspi Publication

Table of Contents

Introduction .... Page 4

Tomi, Nude, After A Bath .... Page 5

In the Bathhouse .... Page 6

Nude Woman After A Bath .... Page 7

Nude Woman Washing Face .... Page 8

Nude Woman Standing and Washing Her Feet .... Page 9

The Grasshopper .... Page 10

Sunlight .... Page 11

Nymphs Hunting .... Page 12

Springtime Lovers .... Page 13

Nude Sitting .... Page 14

The Dawn .... Page 15

A Fairy Under Starry Skies .... Page 16

By Summer Seas .... Page 17

Nude Bathers on Rock at Beach .... Page 18

Diana .... Page 19

The Shepherdess .... Page 20

Dew Spreading Its Pearls on Flowers .... Page 21

Resting Nymphe .... Page 22

Eastern Beauty .... Page 23

Pool in Harem .... Page 24

Pool in Harem Whiskey Advertisement .... Page 25

Bath In Harem .... Page 26

Odalisque with Slave .... Page 27

Greek Woman at Bath .... Page 28

The Japanese Toilette .... Page 29

A Favorite Custom .... Page 30

The Goddess Diana with Hunting Dog .... Page 31

Artemis Goddess of the Hunt .... Page 32

The Shipwrecked Man and the Sea .... Page 33

Cupid and Psyche .... Page 34

Parau na te Varua ino or Words of the Devil .... Page 35
Salome, The Stomach Dance .... Page 36
Nude Woman Reflected in Pond .... Page 37
Judith .... Page 38
The Dancer .... Page 39
Two Friends .... Page 40
Eve and Adam .... Page 41
Psyche and Pan .... Page 42
Nude Woman with Chestnut Hair .... Page 43
Nude Woman In Werner's Rowing Boat .... Page 44
The Young Bather .... Page 45
Nude Princess of India .... Page 46
Love Nymph .... Page 47
Madonna .... Page 48
A Seated Female .... Page 49
Nude Asleep on Bed .... Page 50
Nude Sitting on Edge of Bed .... Page 51
Nude Woman Seated at Dressing Table .... Page 52
Nude Girl .... Page 53
The Turkish Bath .... Page 54
Nude Pregnant Woman with Shadow .... Page 55
Nude Woman Sitting with Flowers .... Page 56
Nude Woman with Arm Across Forehead .... Page 57
Nude From Behind .... Page 58
About the Author .... Page 59
Other Books by the Author Available on Amazon .... Page 59

Introduction

The female nude form continuously fascinates us and has since time immemorial. I have been married for 27 years and I am still fascinated by my wife when she disrobes.

In the past, depending upon the society and the times, seeing images of the nude female body, let alone the body itself, has been restricted to the rich. Social taboos and religious taboos have often obscured the female form (and male form, too) from general public view. Thankfully, artists, within such societies of the past and of today, have preserved for all of us the ever changing beauty that is woman.

Of course, today's world is filled with actual presentations of naked women and men – in movies, cable TV shows and a multitude of publications. Cameras are everywhere and private nude photos fill digital archives. Despite the wide spread availability of real nude imagery, there is still a constant craving for artistic nudes. These may come in the form of nicely crafted fantasy sex scenes in movies, but graphic novels and paintings are also a major source that fulfills our cultural need for seeing the artistic female nude.

This book provides a selection of artistic female nudes before the Internet, movies, graphic novels and TV were a part of our culture. It was also a time before everyone had a camera. The paintings and art that follow represent a time when daring artists created works to fascinate us and, at times, shock us with naked women.

Some of the artists presented here will be familiar to you, but I have also tried to select artists whose work will be both new to you and yet still provide a pleasant surprise of artistic discovery.

Tomi, Nude, After A Bath by Goyo Hashiguchi

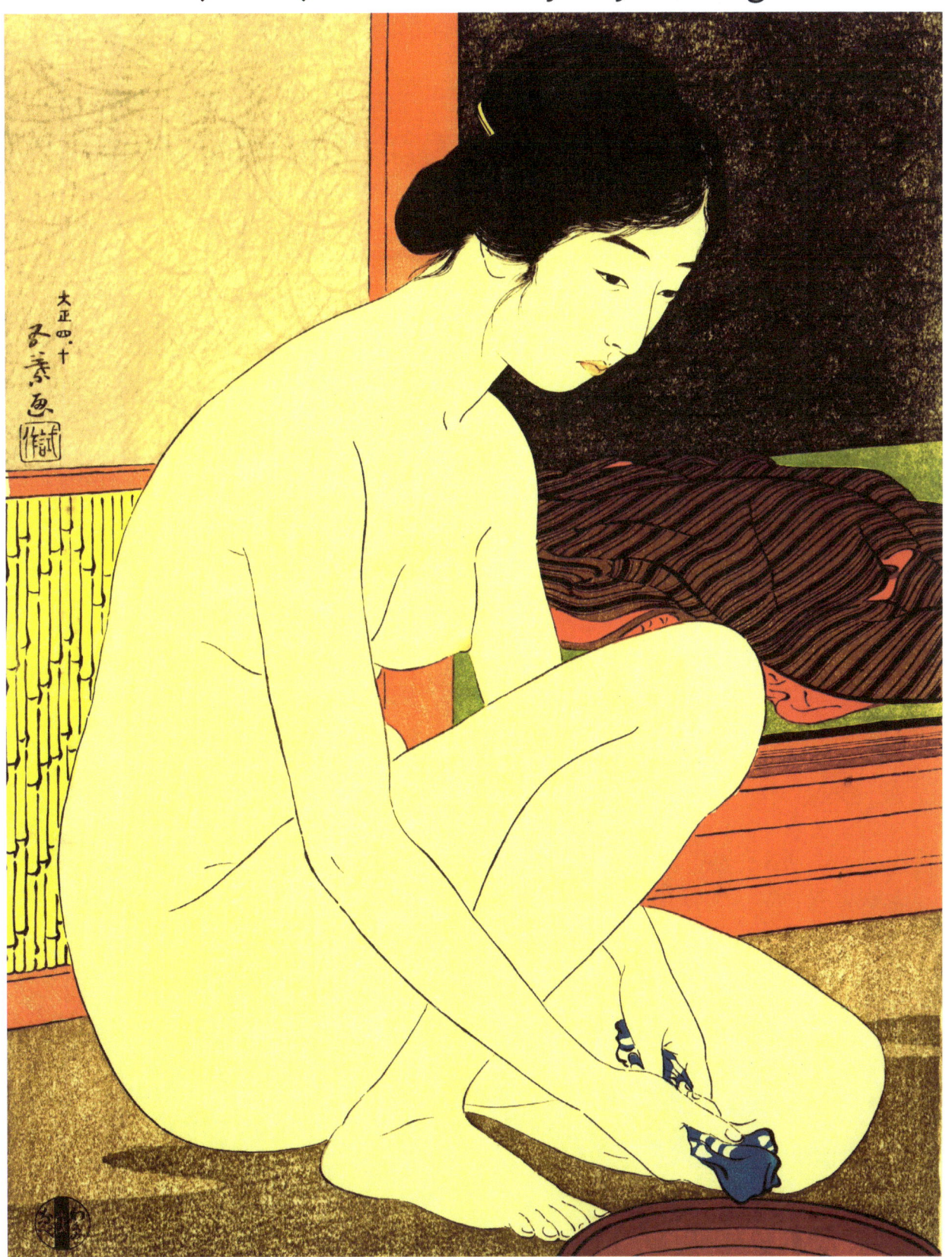

In the Bathhouse by Torii Kiyonaga

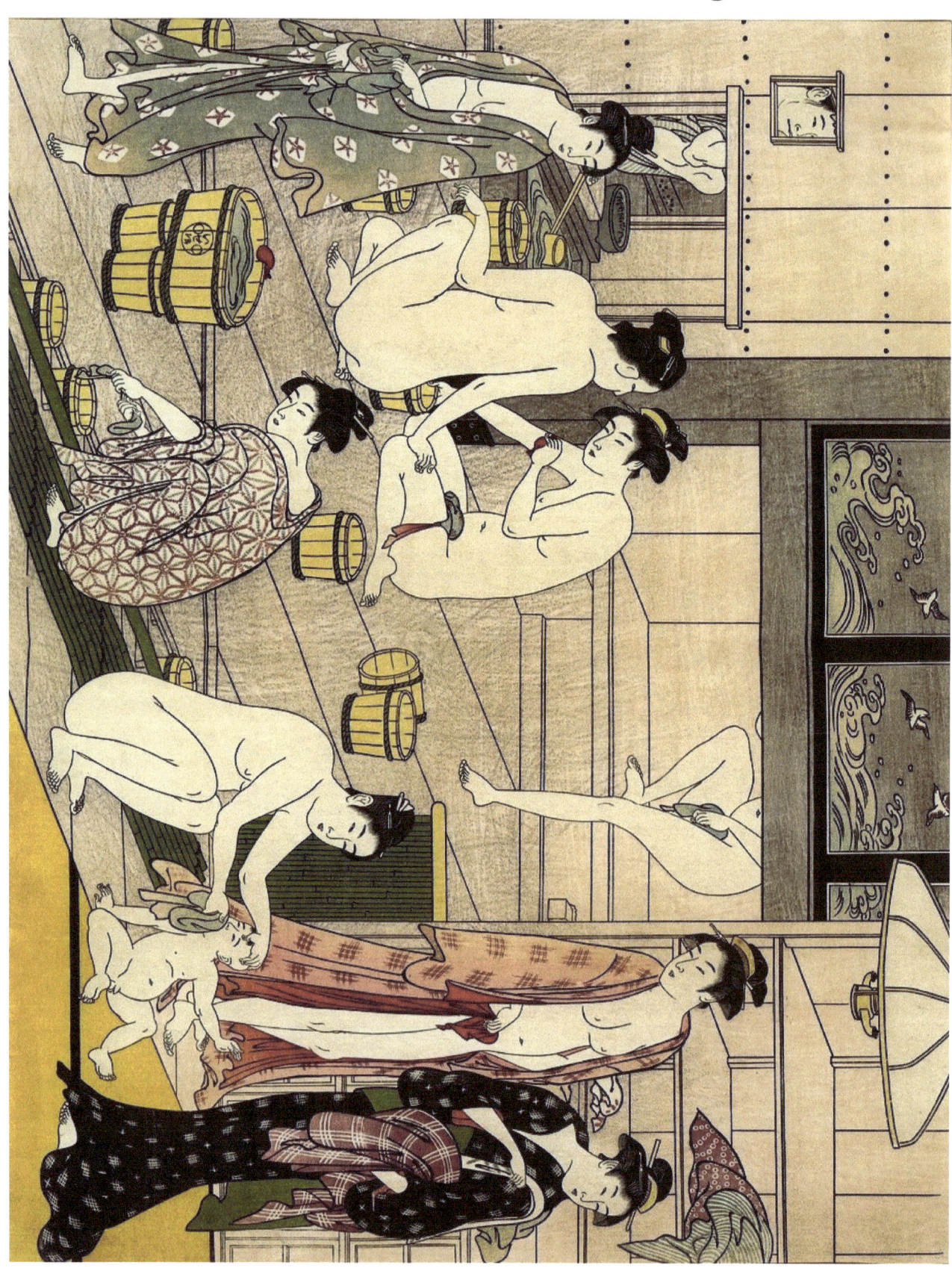

Nude Woman After A Bath by Goyo Hasiguchi

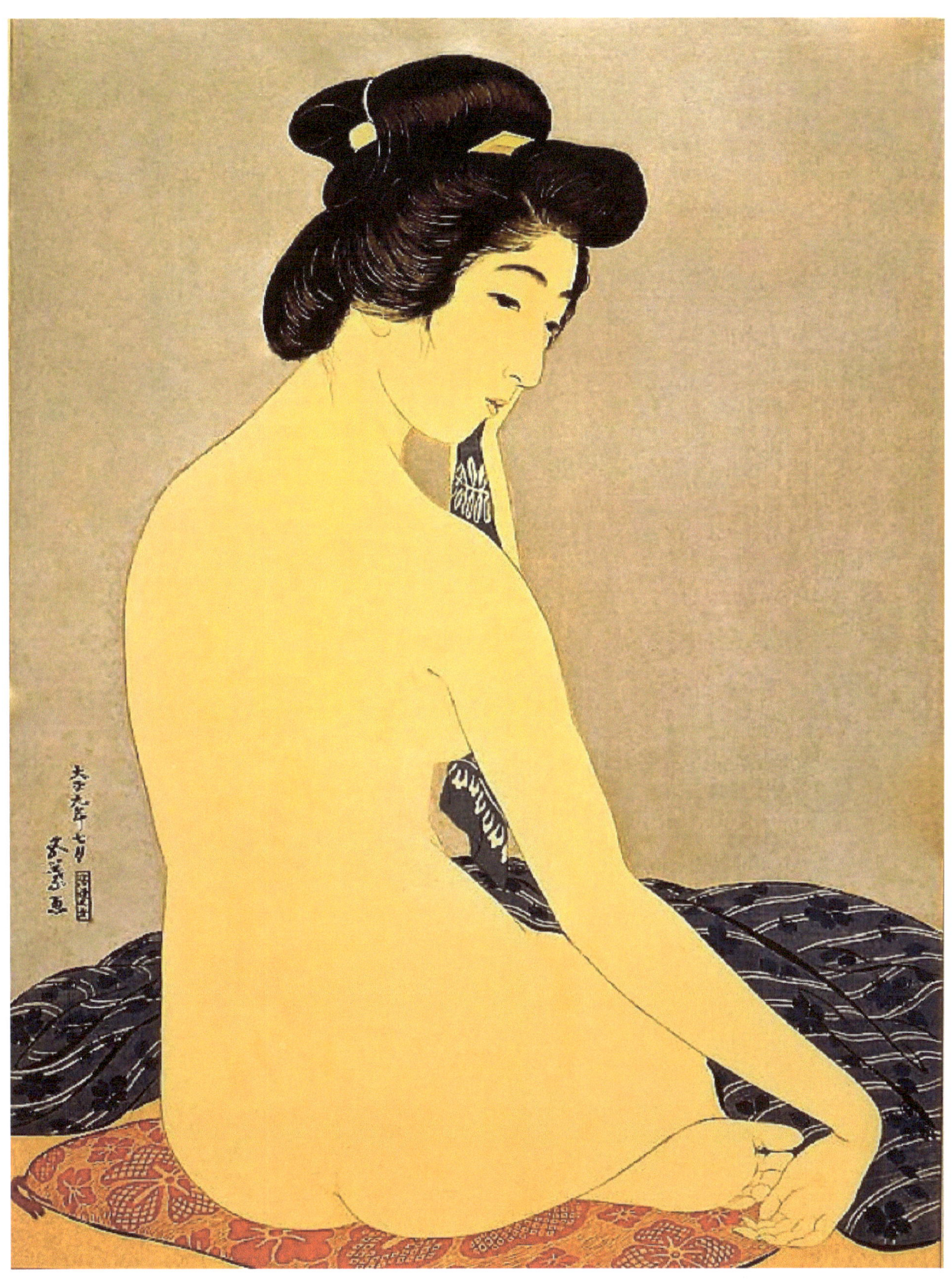

Nude Woman Washing Face by Goyo Hasiguchi

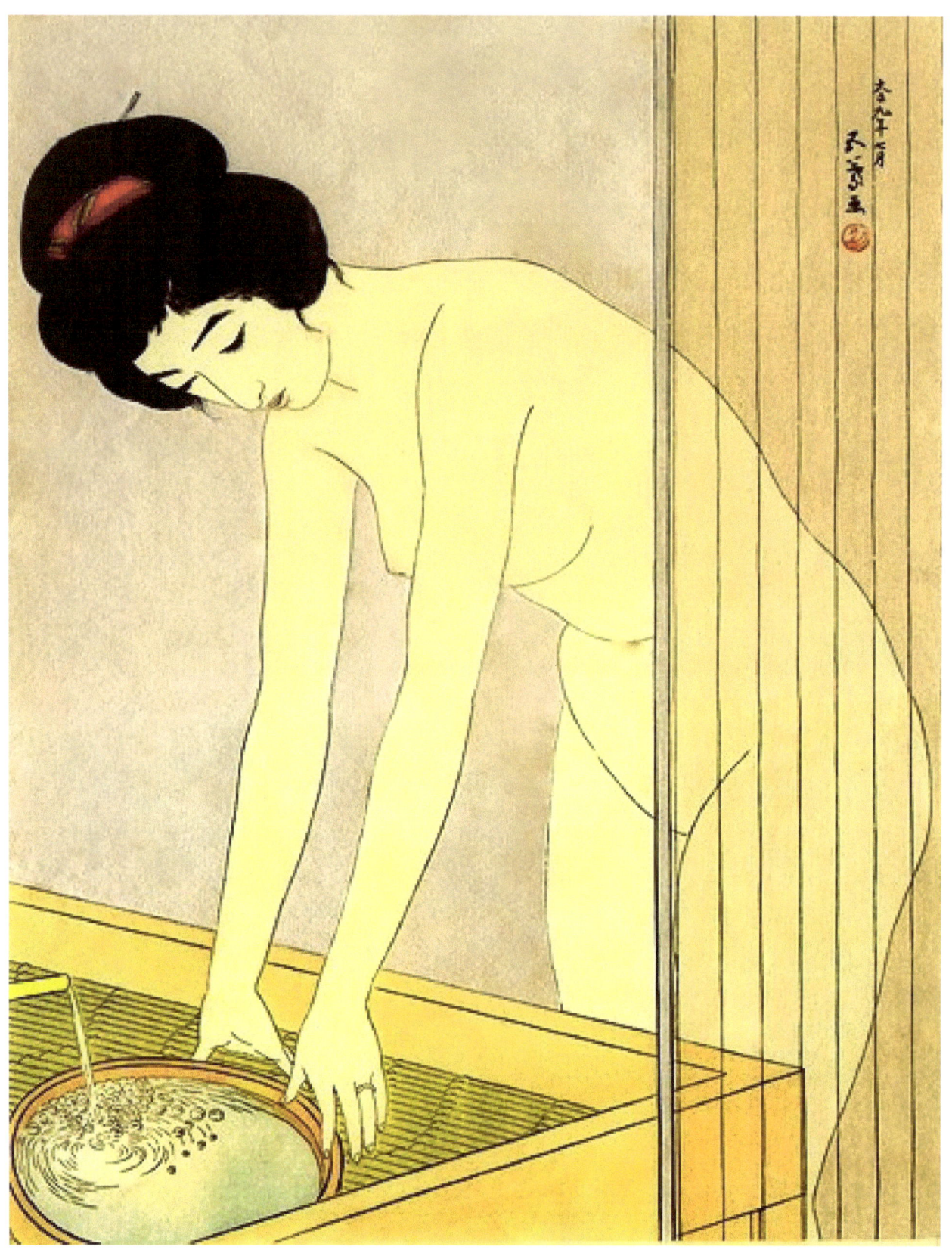

Nude Washing Her Feet by Goyo Hashiguchi

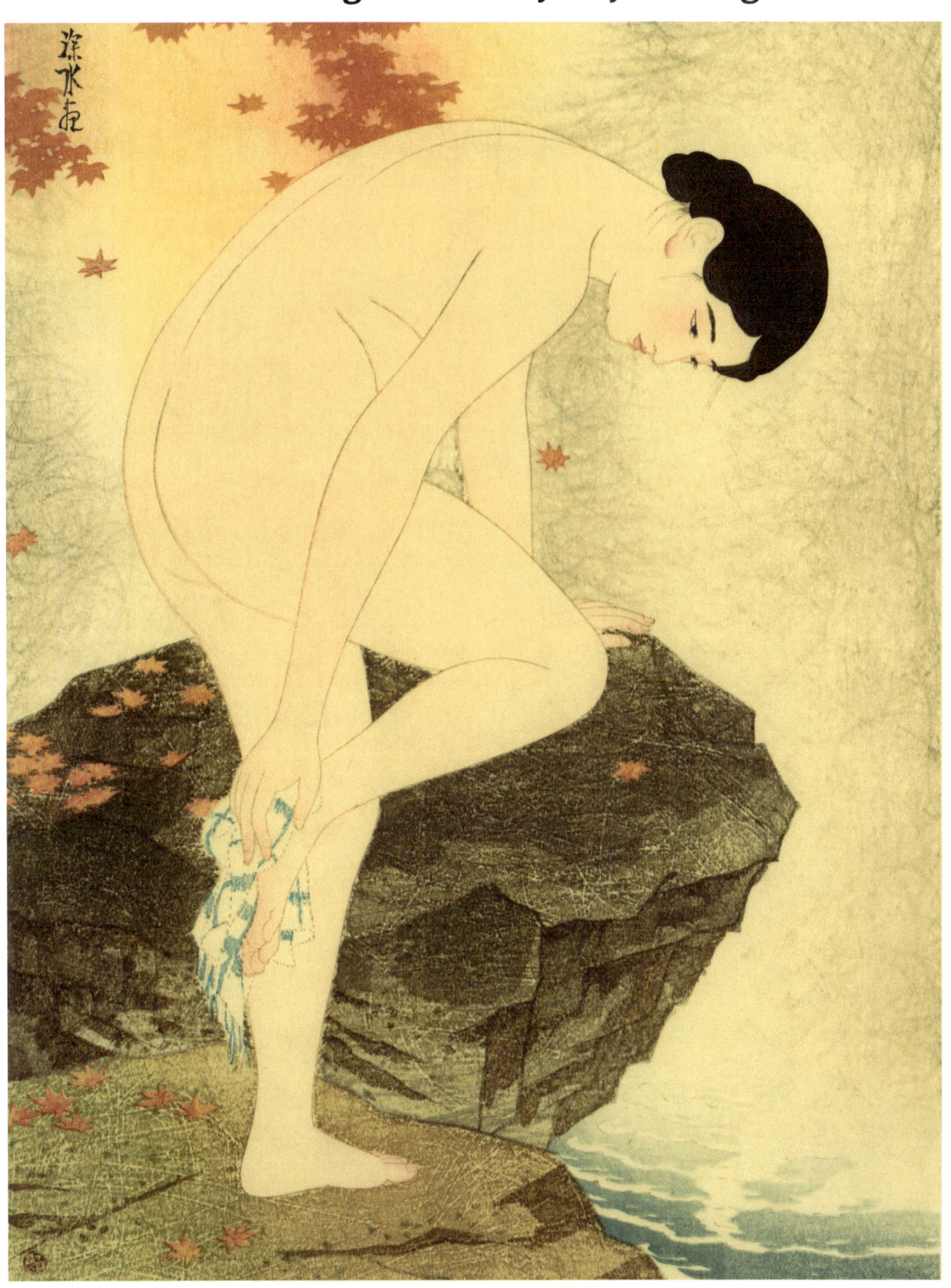

The Grasshopper by Jules-Joseph Lefebvre

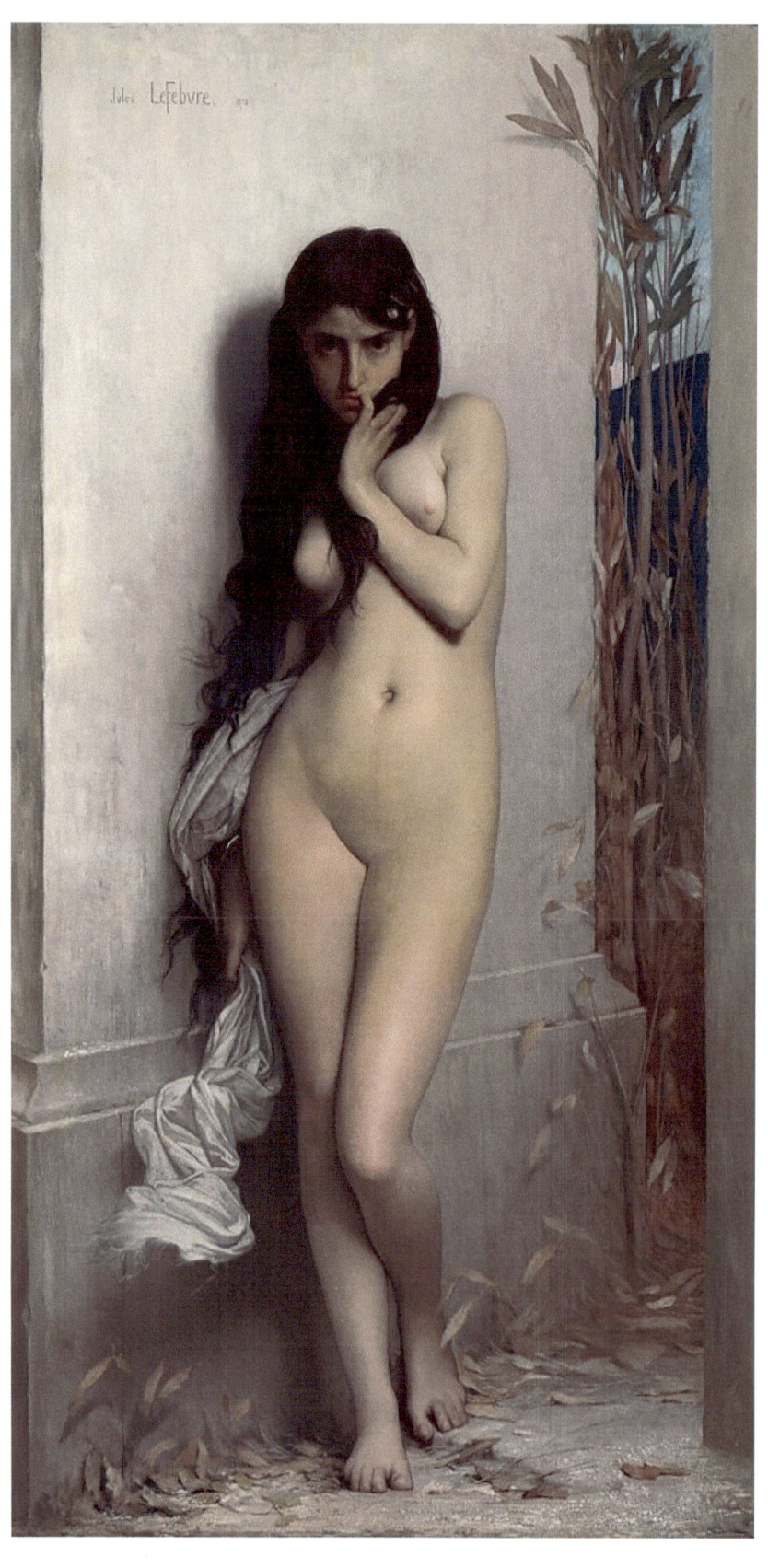

Sunlight by Julius LeBlanc Stewart

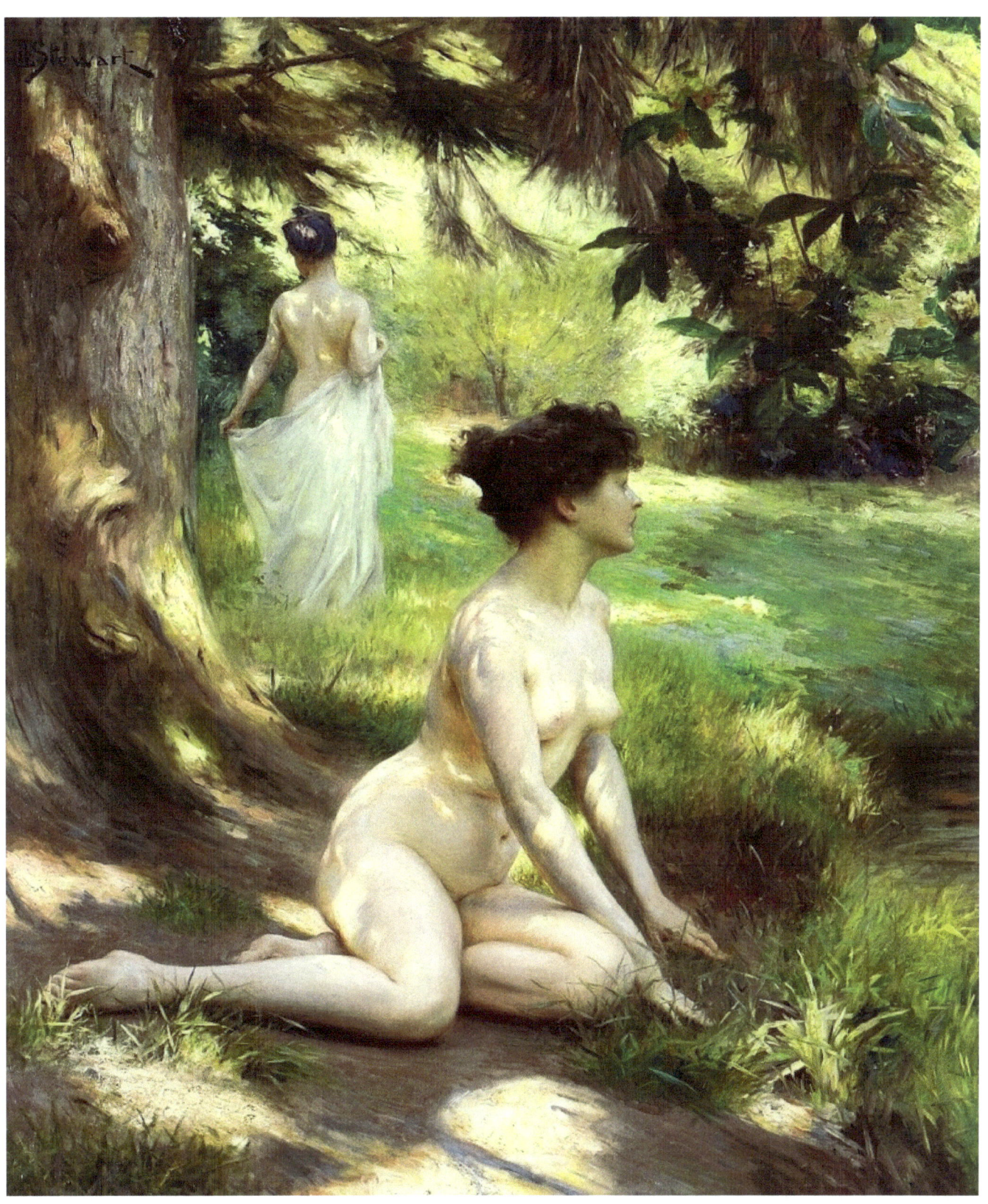

Nymphs Hunting by Julius LeBlanc Stewart

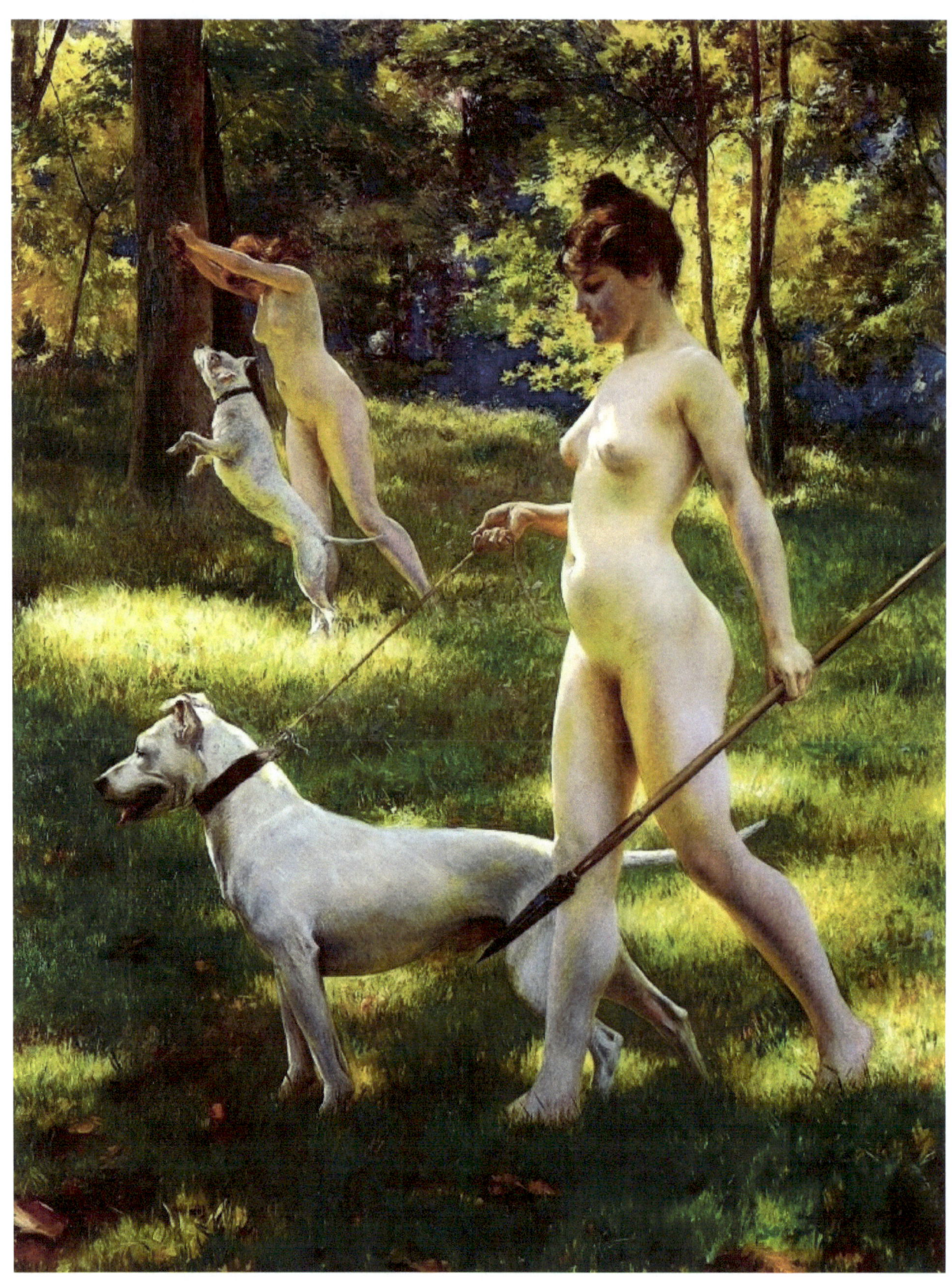

Springtime Lovers - Chinese Erotic Art

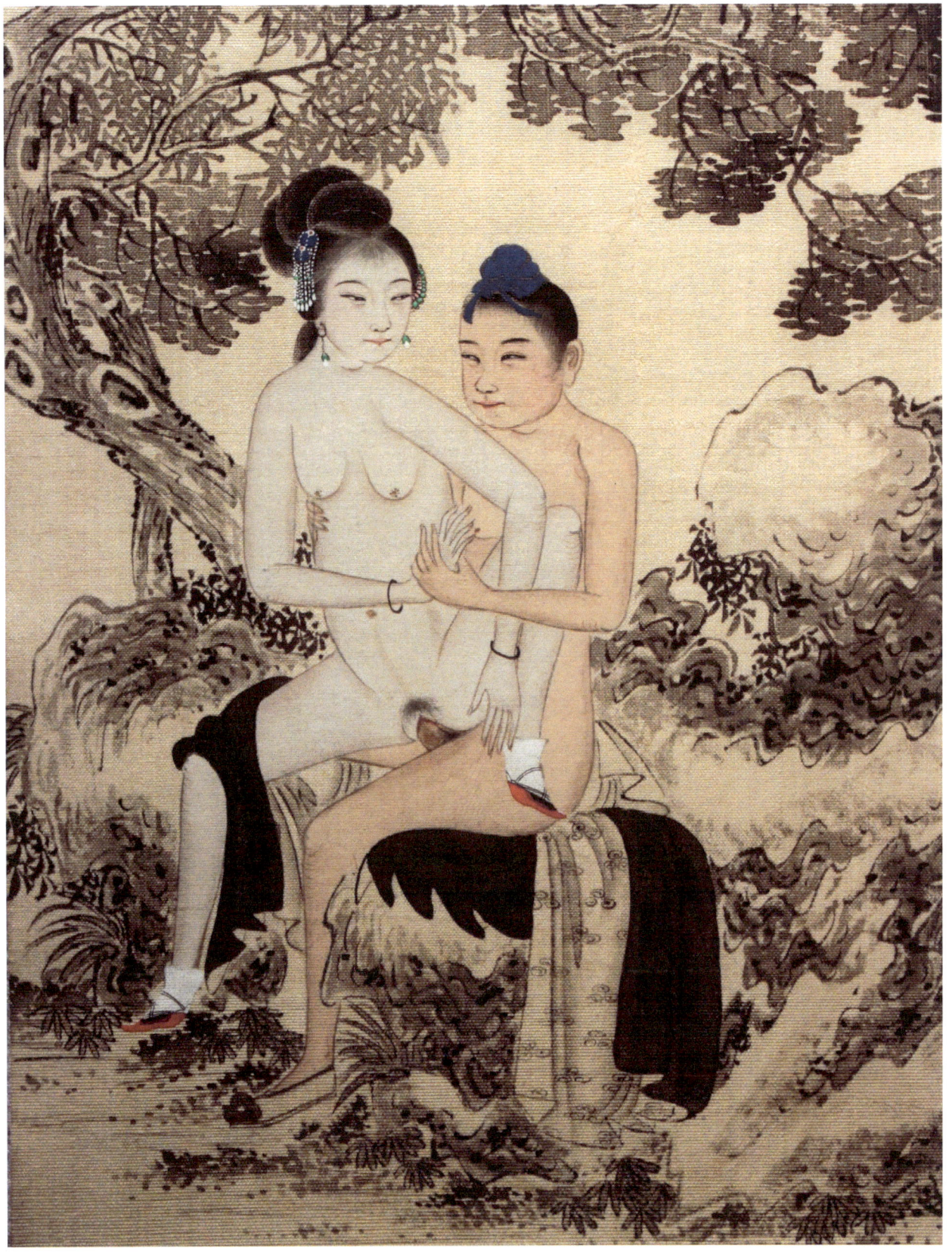

Nude Sitting by Amedeo Modigliani

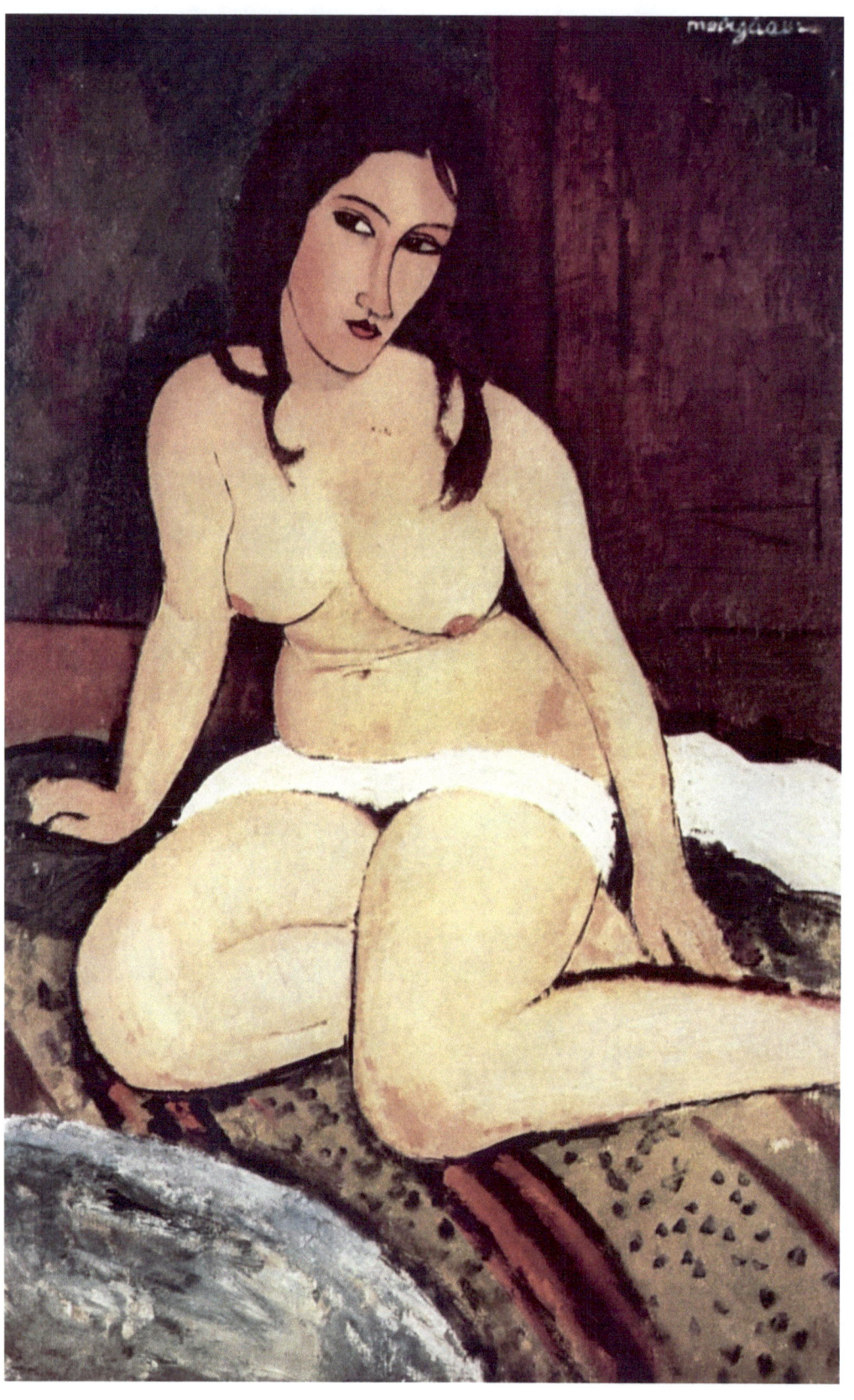

The Dawn by Luis Ricardo Falero

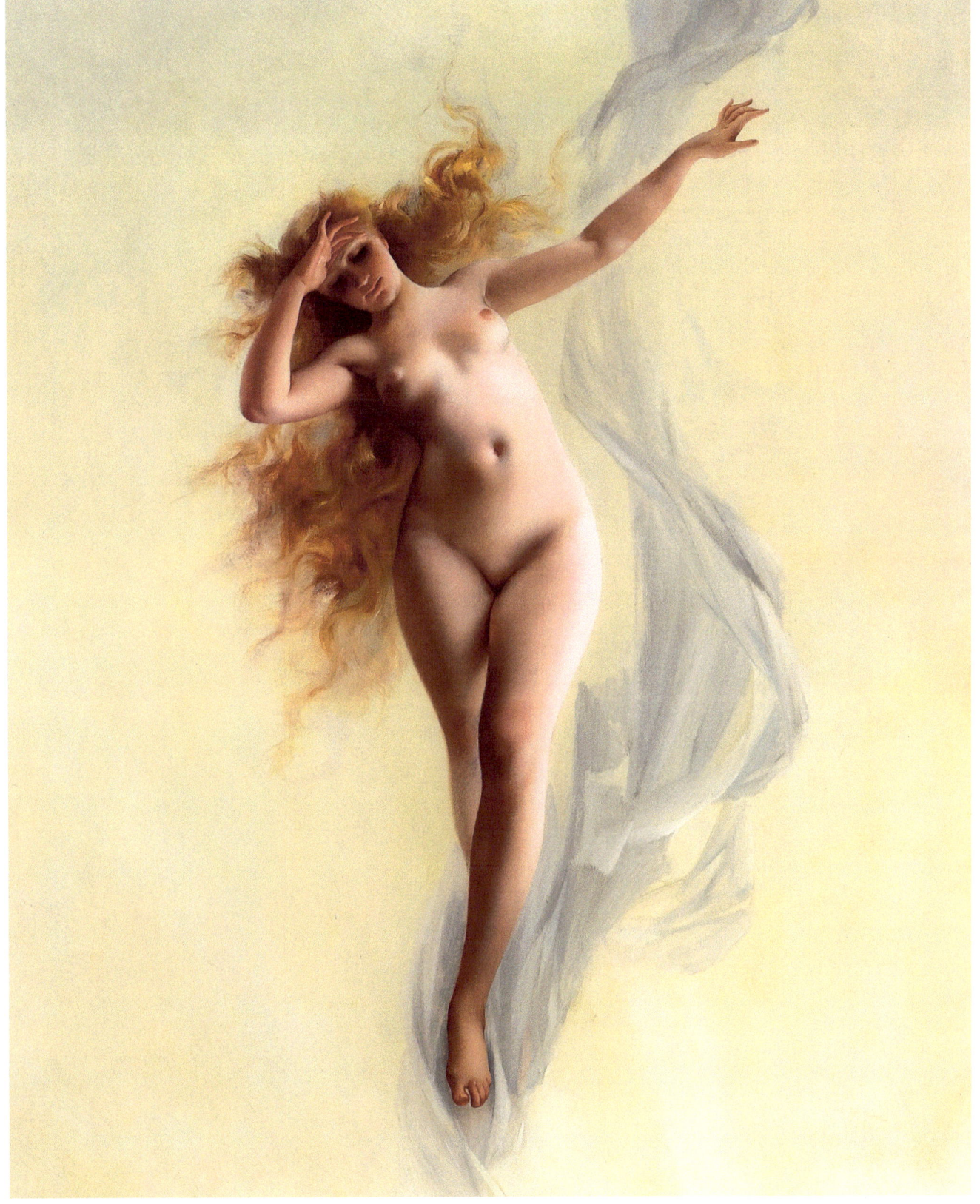

A Fairy Under Starry Skies by Luis Ricardo Falero

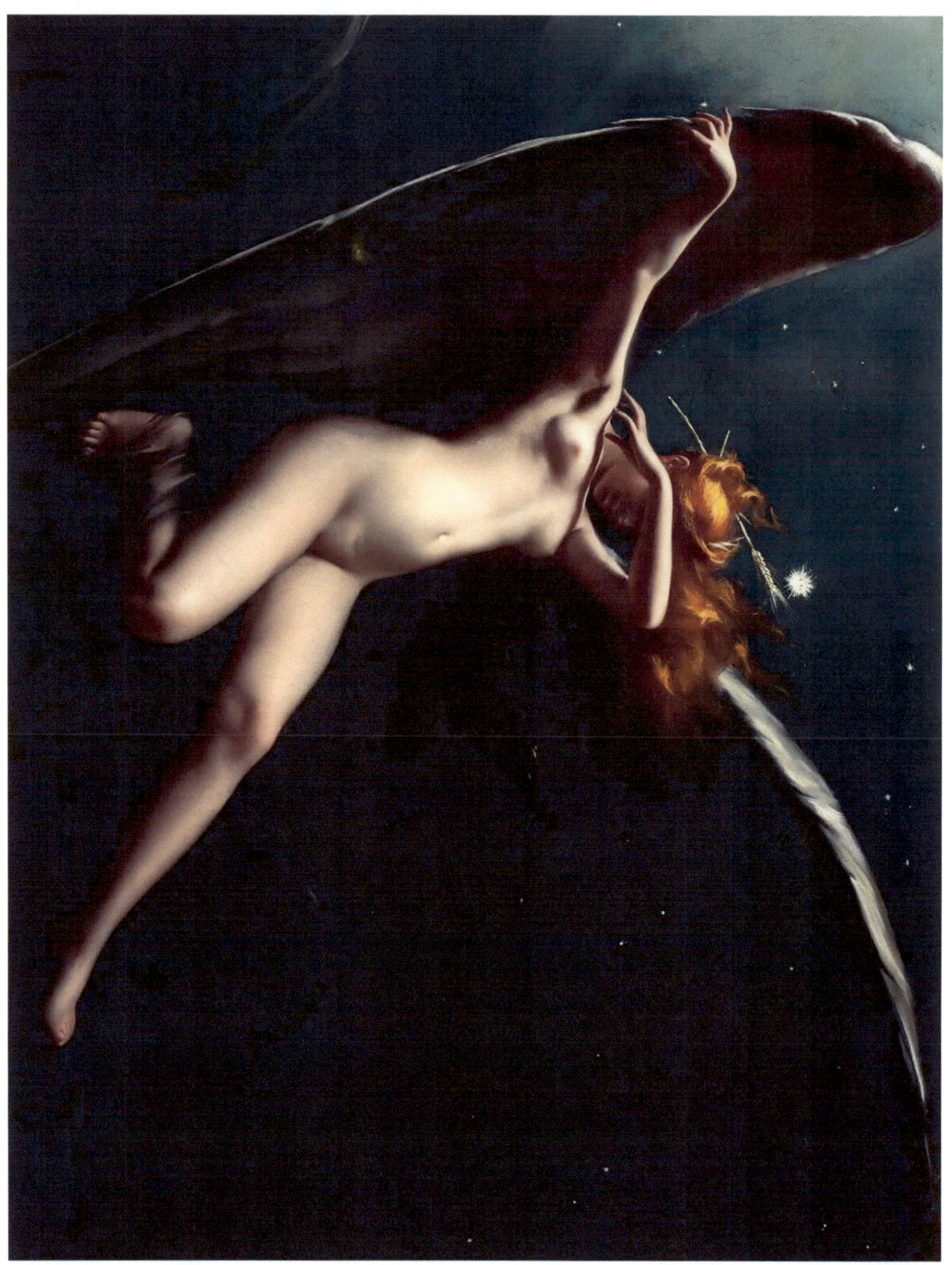

By Summer Seas by Herbert James Draper

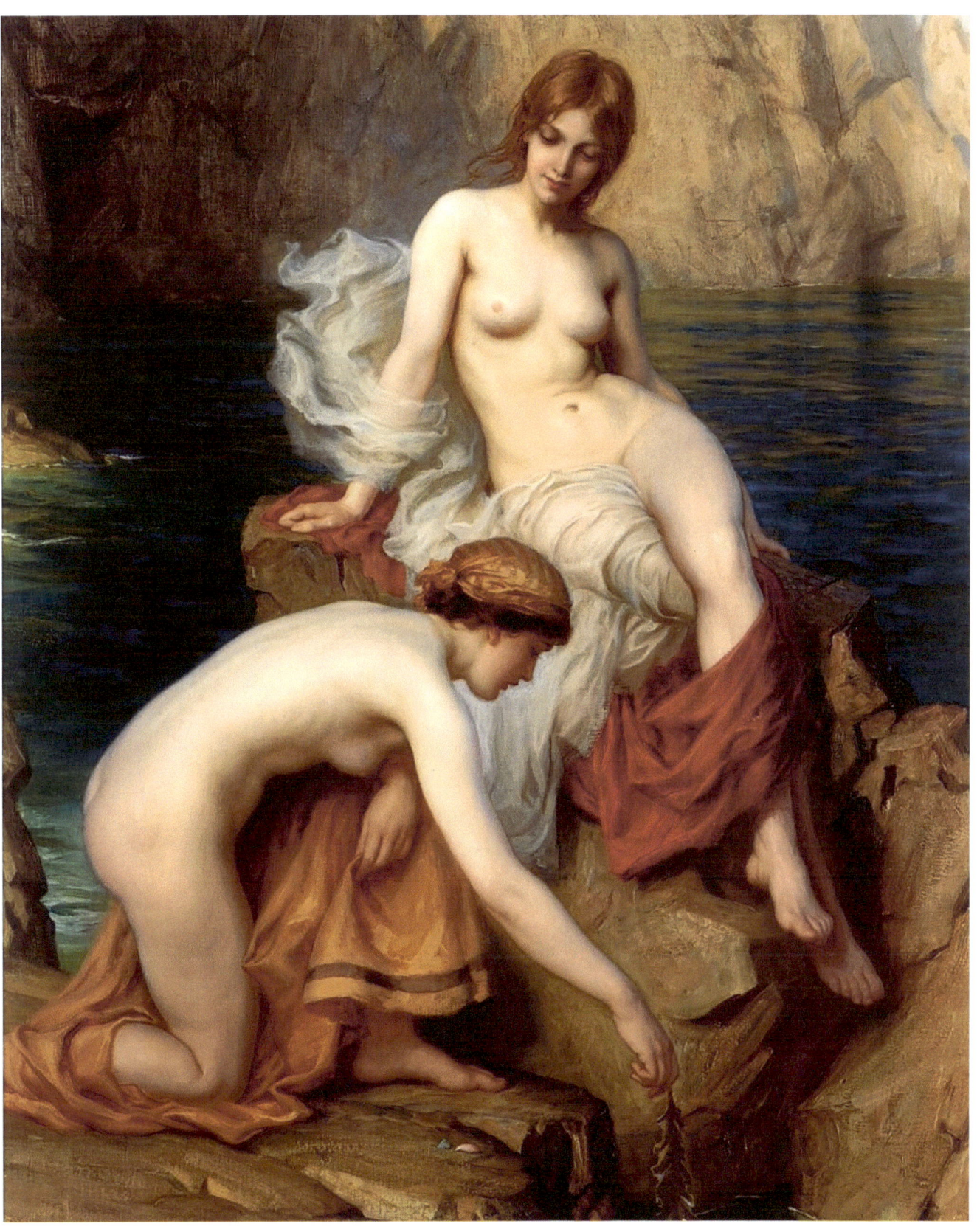

Nude Bathers on Rock at Beach by William Adolphe Bouguereau

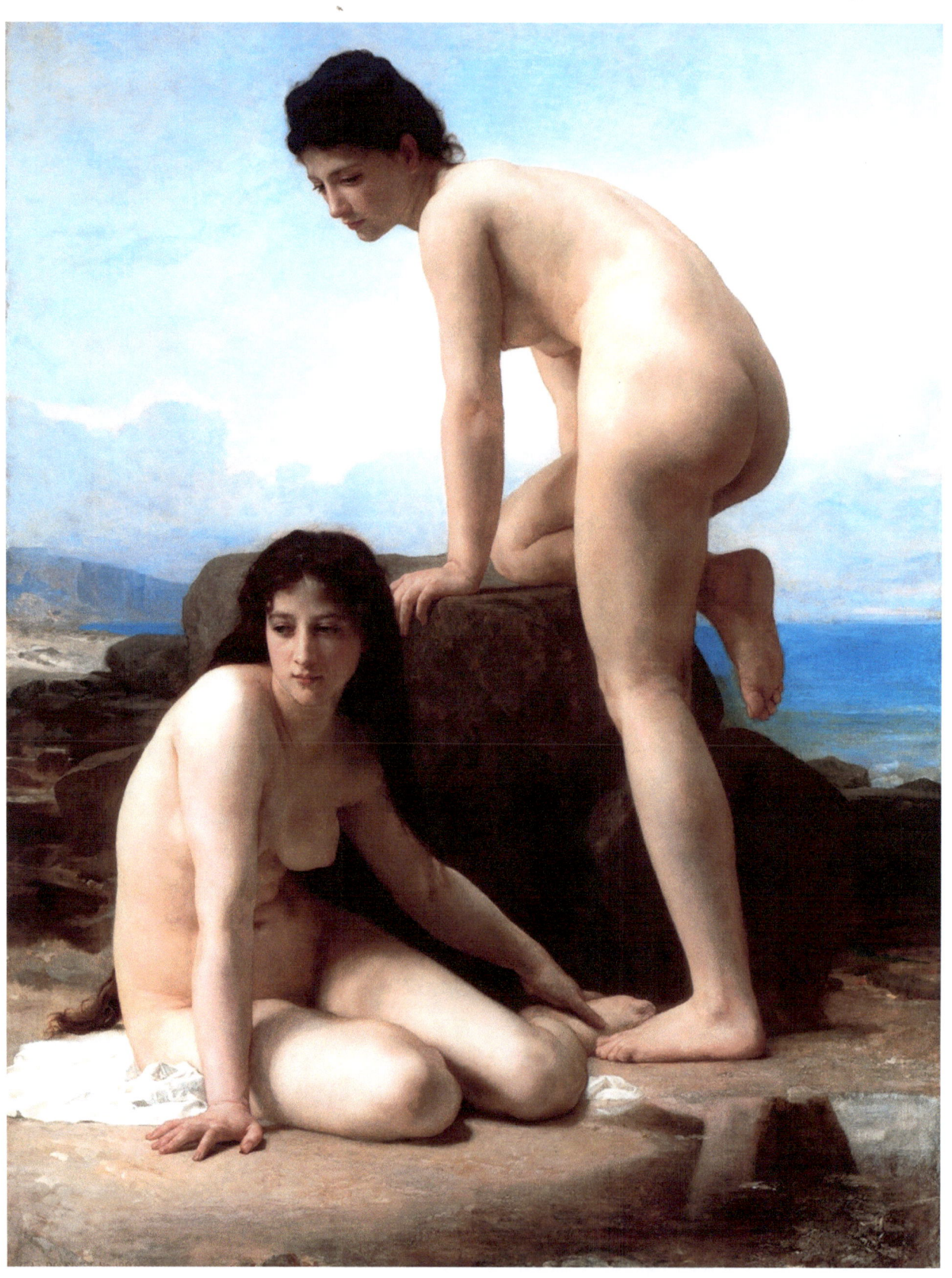

Diana by Jules-elie Delaunay

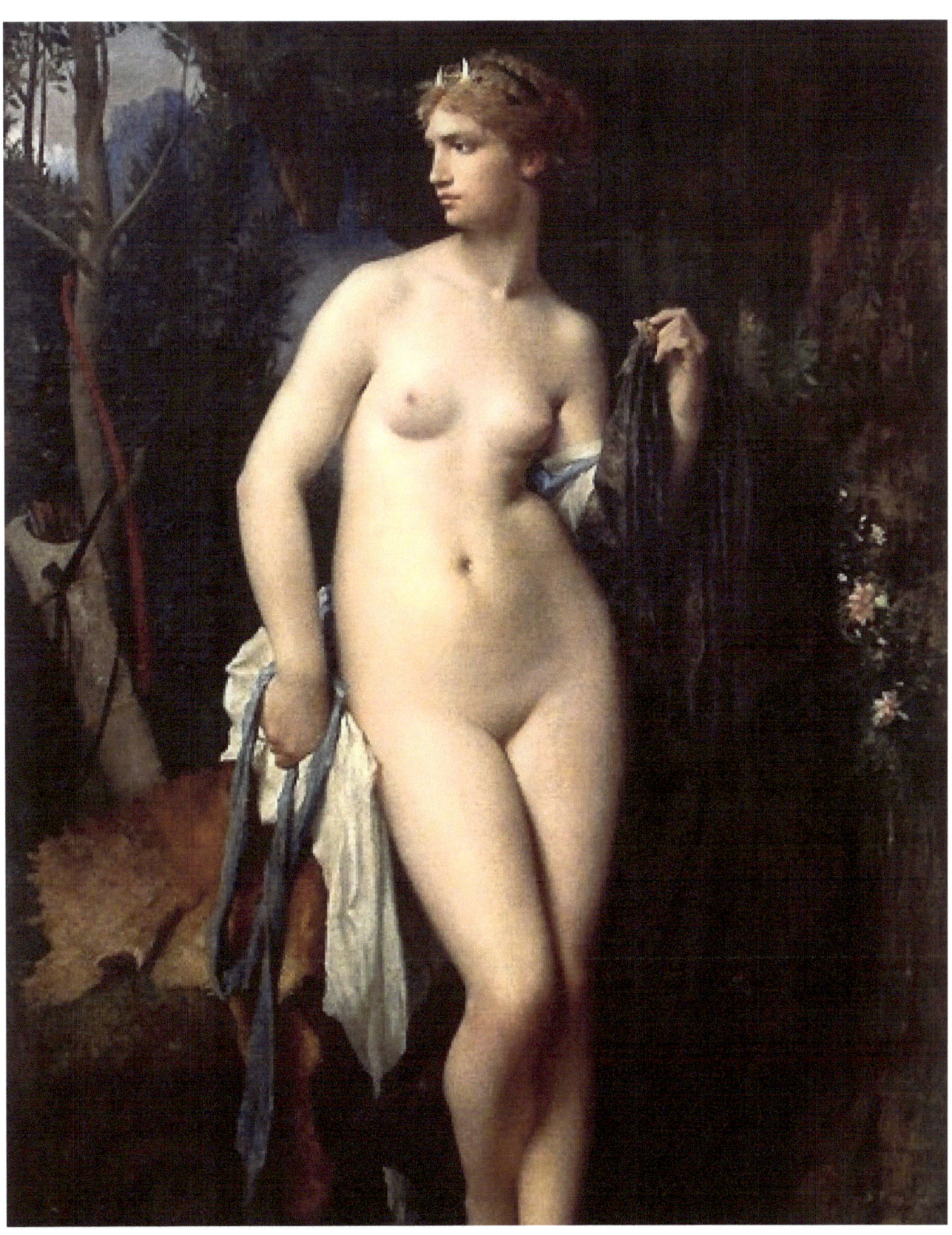

The Shepherdess by Herbert James Draper

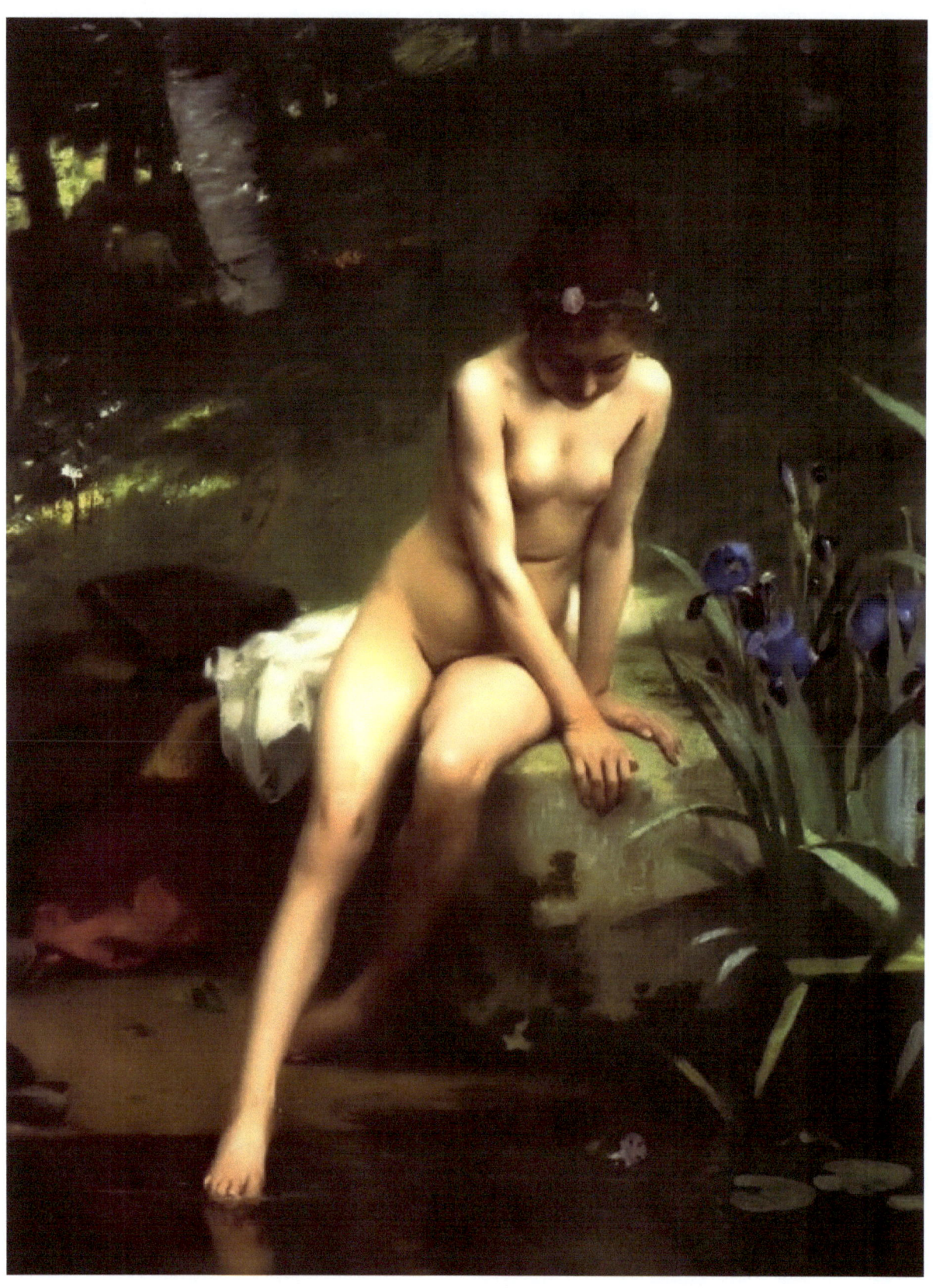

Dew Spreading Its Pearls on Flowers by Jules-Claude Ziegler

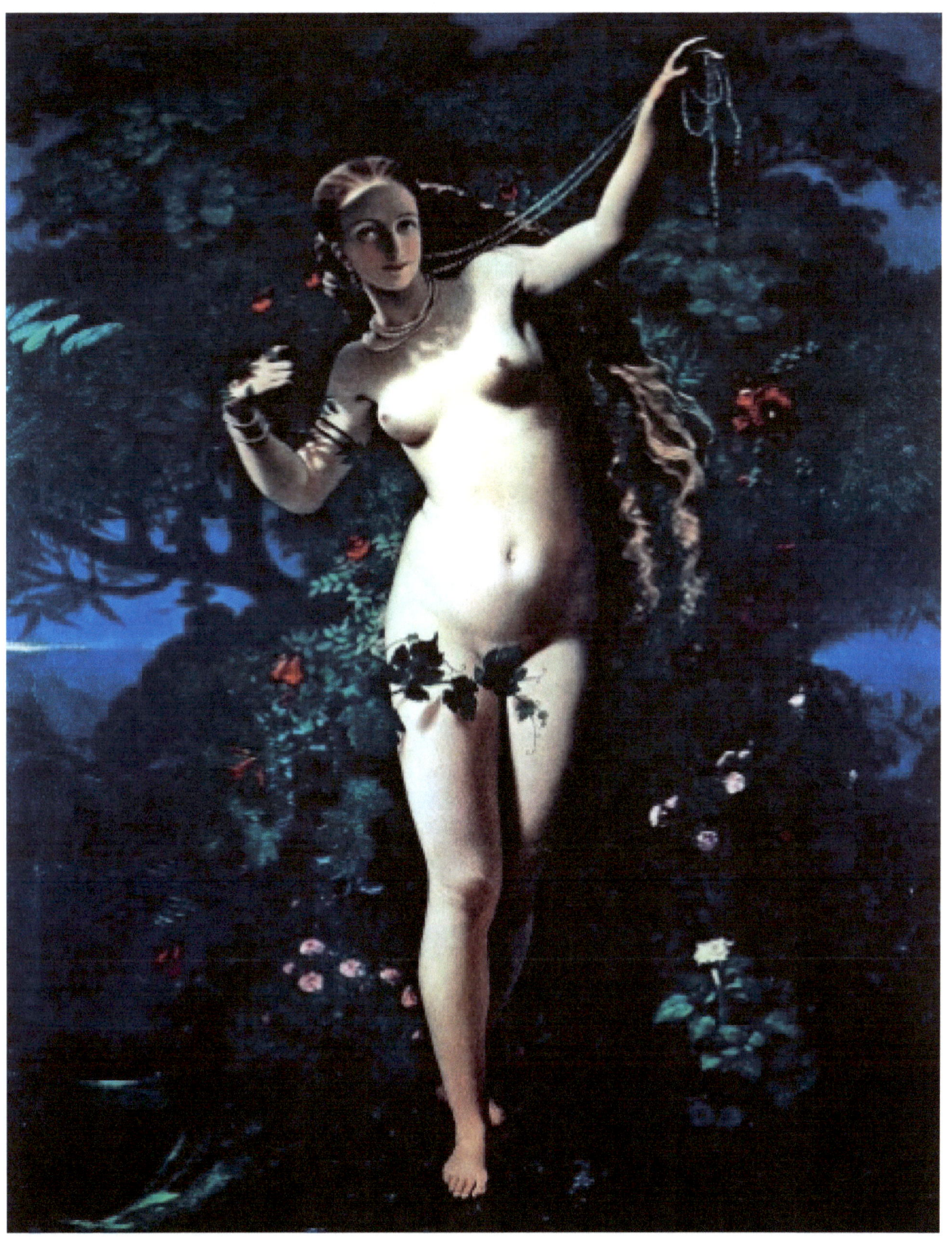

Resting Nymphe by Anselm Feuerbach

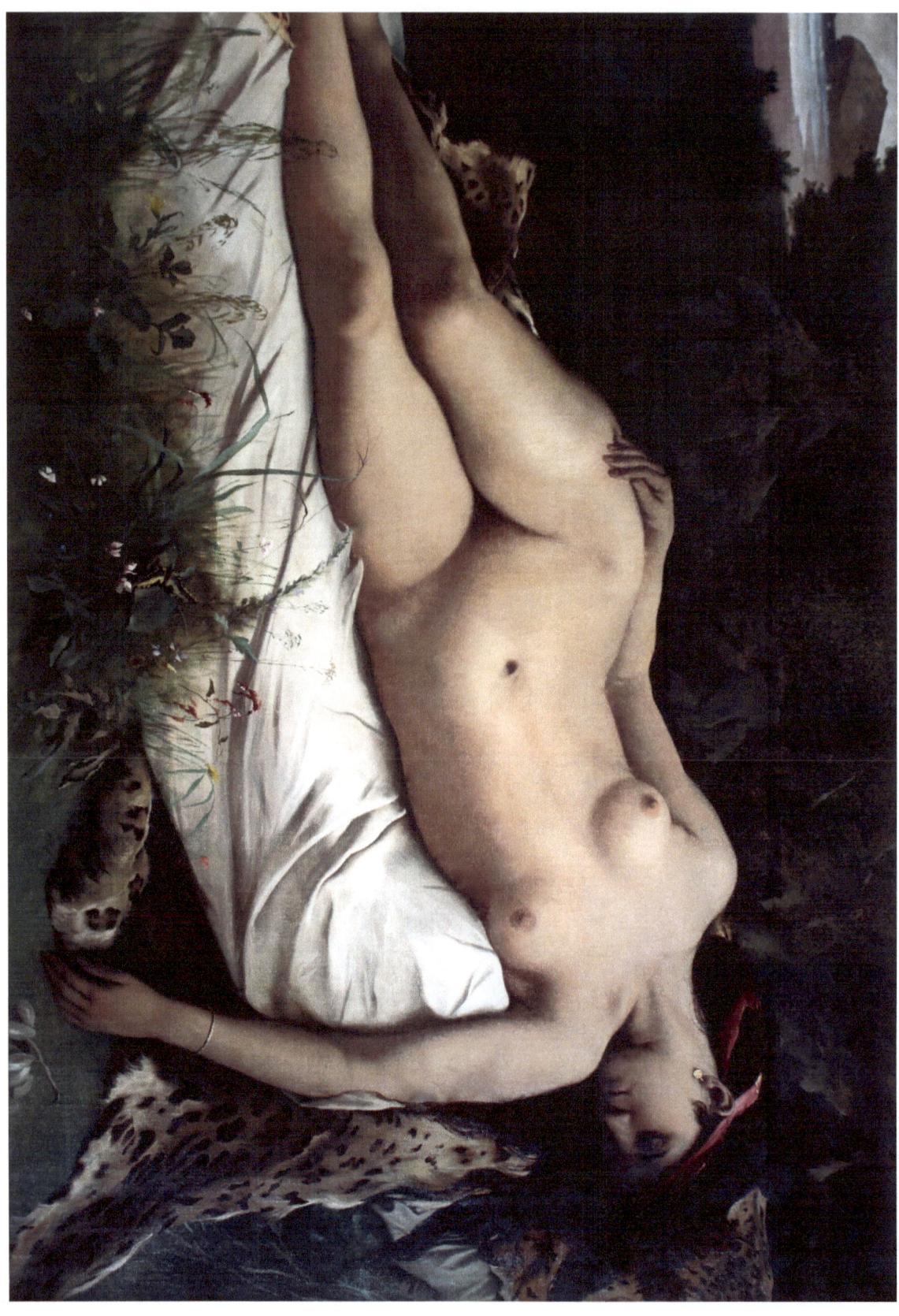

Eastern Beauty by Luis Ricardo Falero

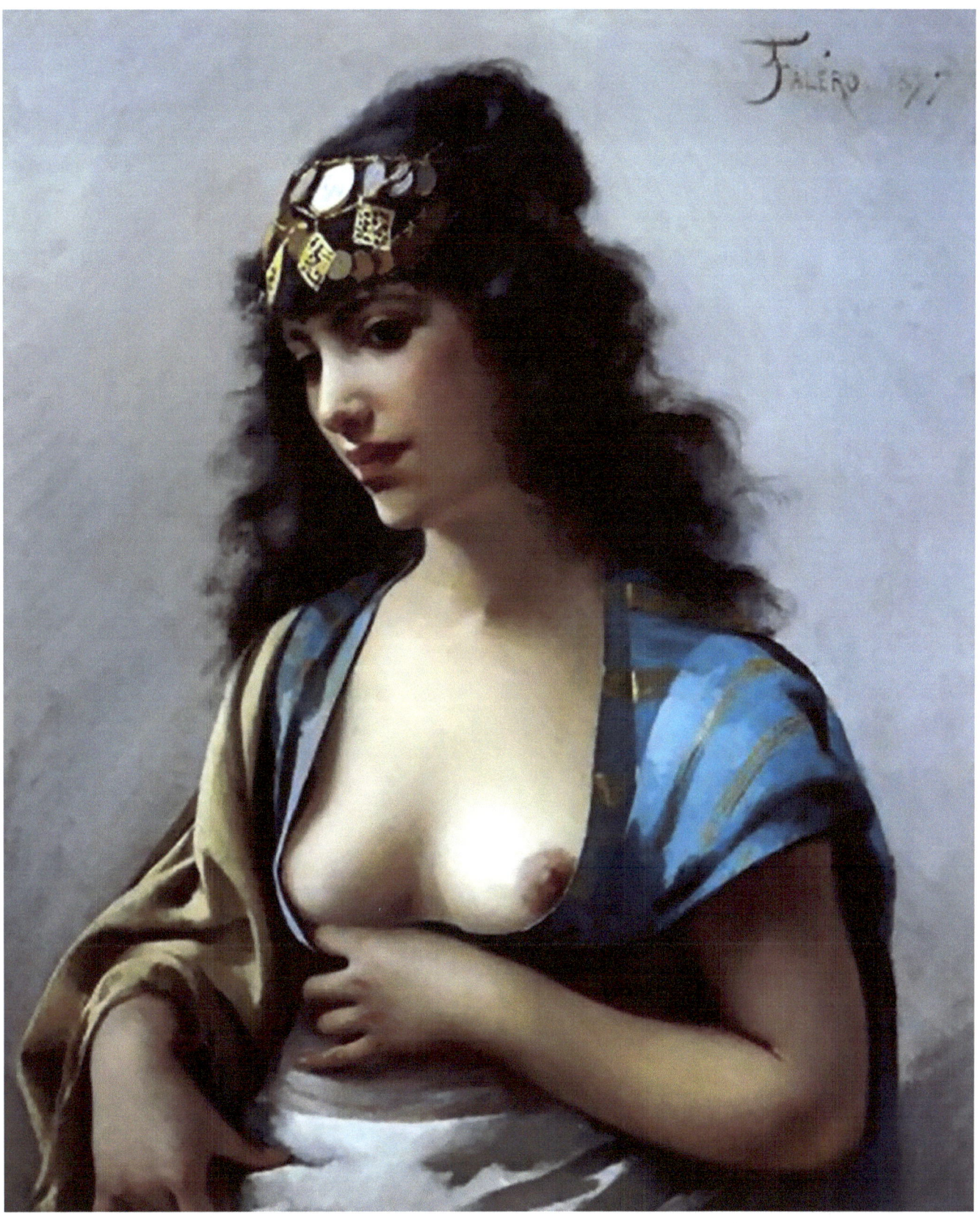

Pool in Harem by Jean Leon Gerome

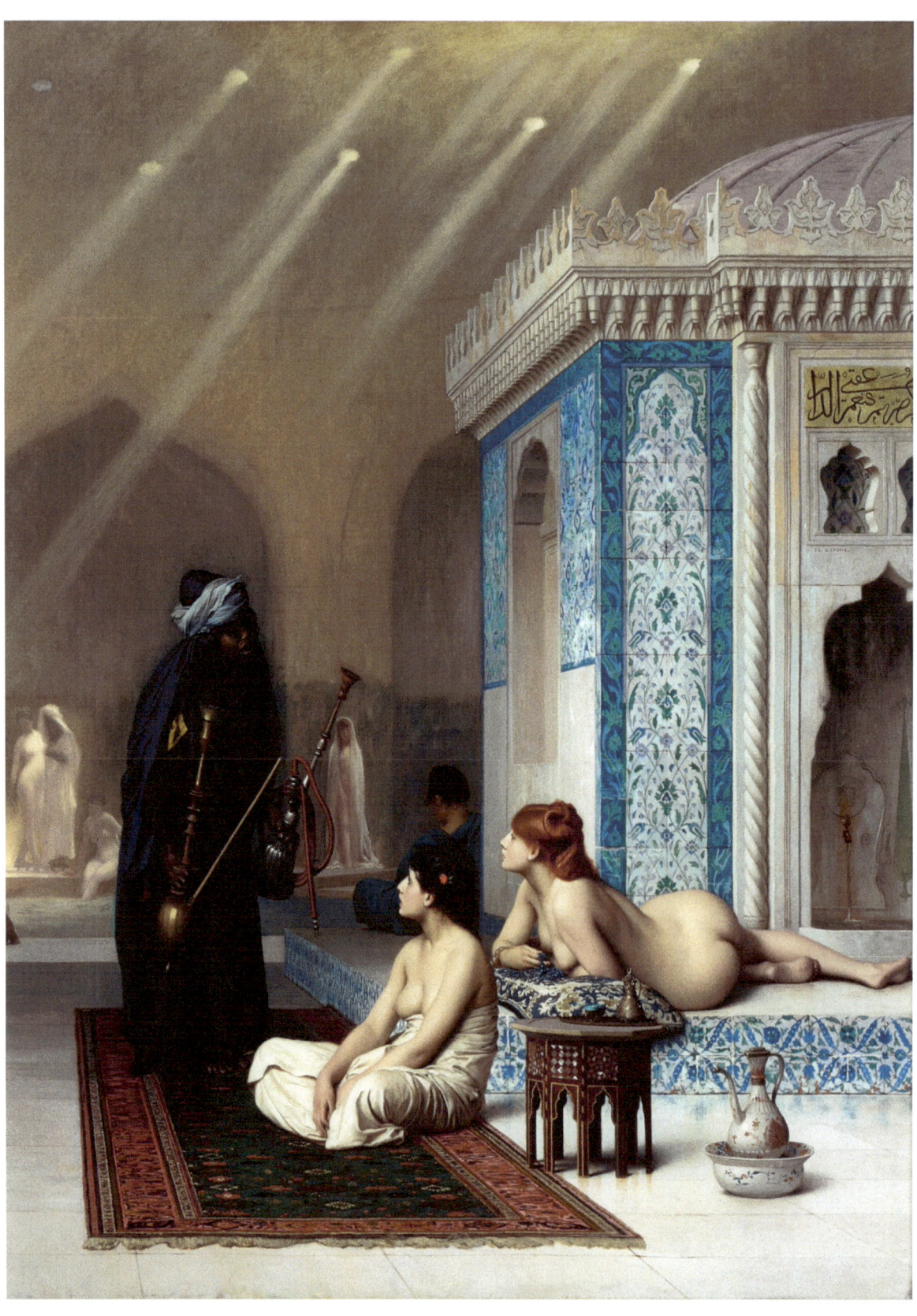

Pool in Harem Whiskey Advertisement by Jean Leon Gerome

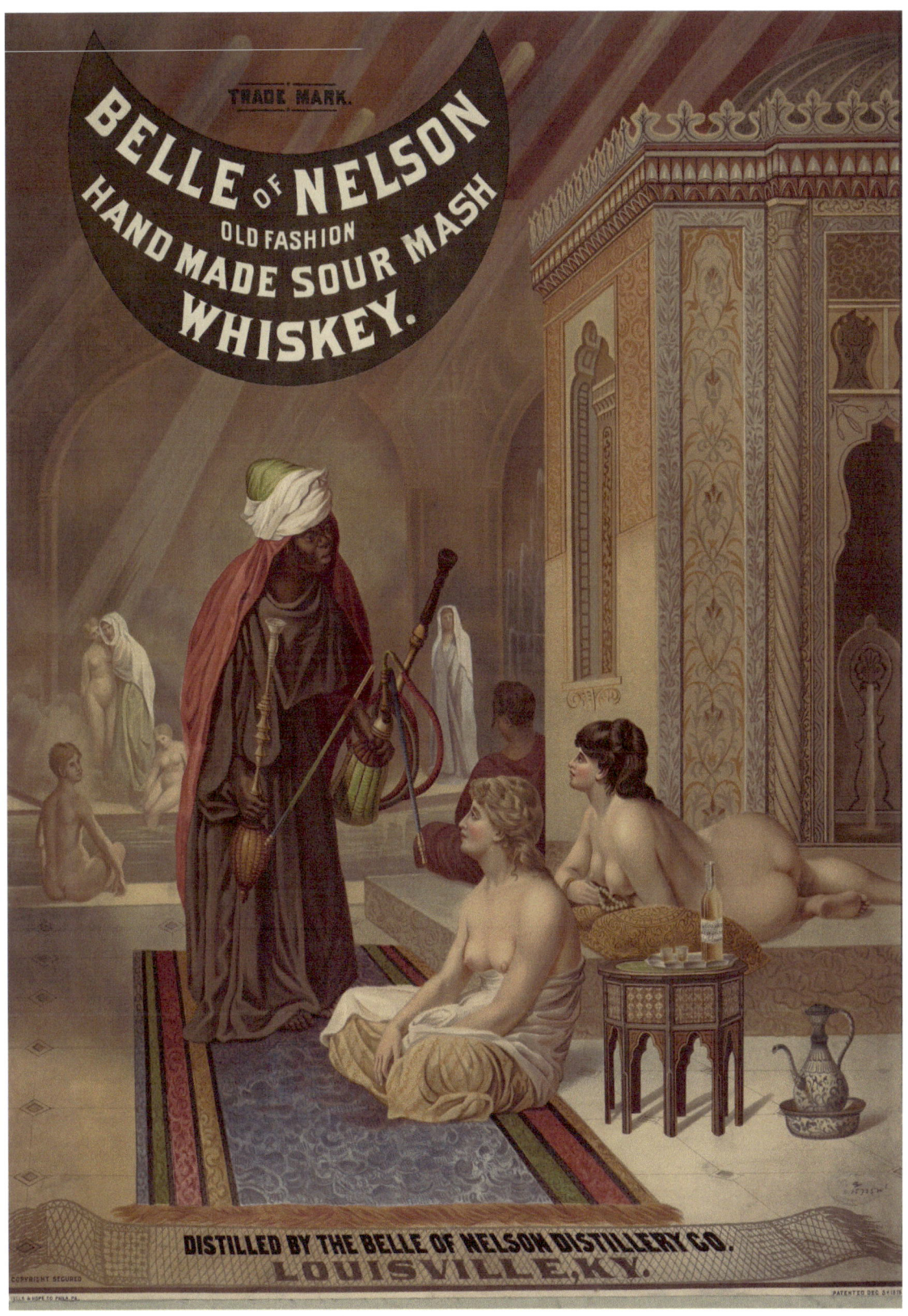

Bath In Harem by Jean Léon Gérome

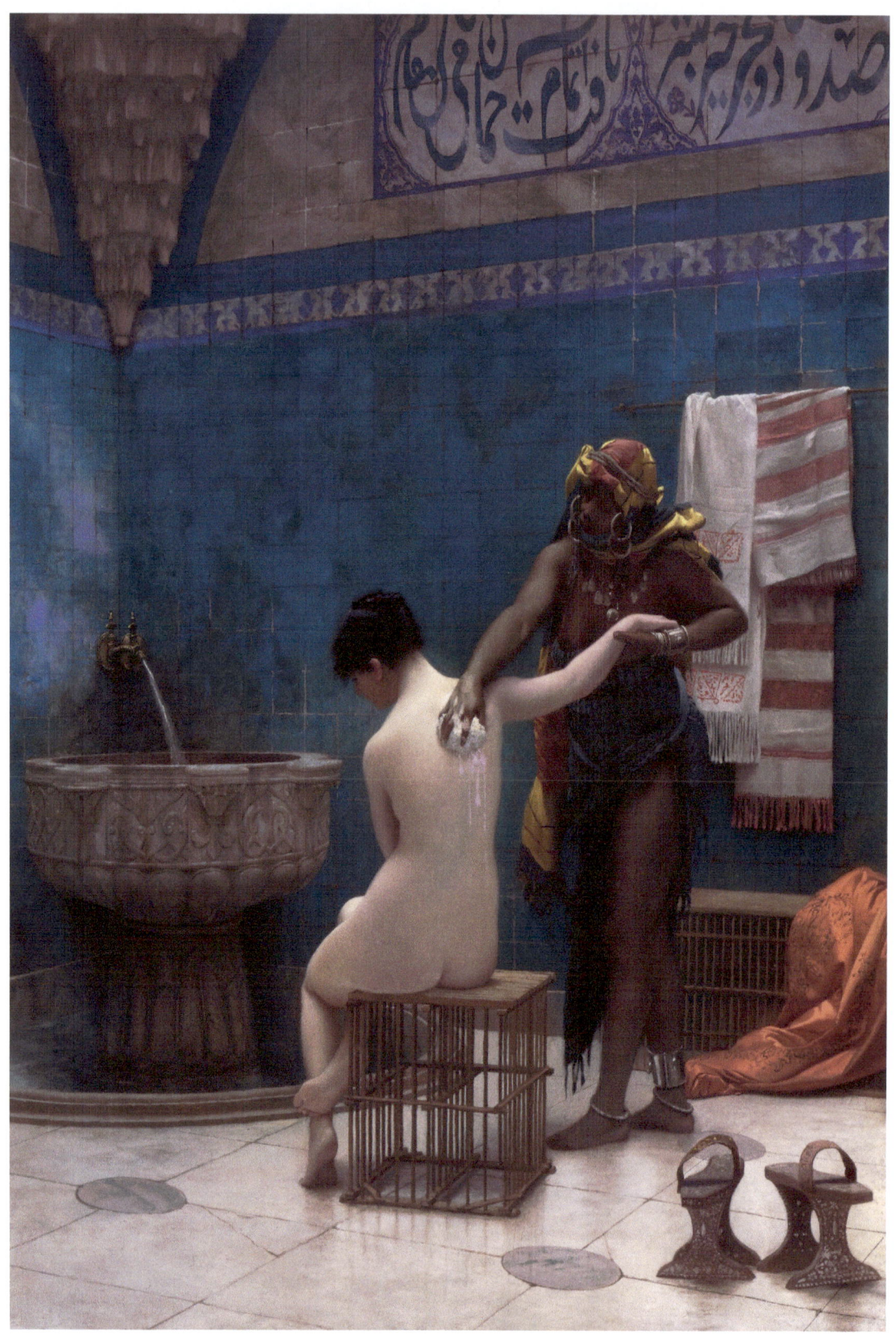

Odalisque with Slave by Jean Paul Flandrin

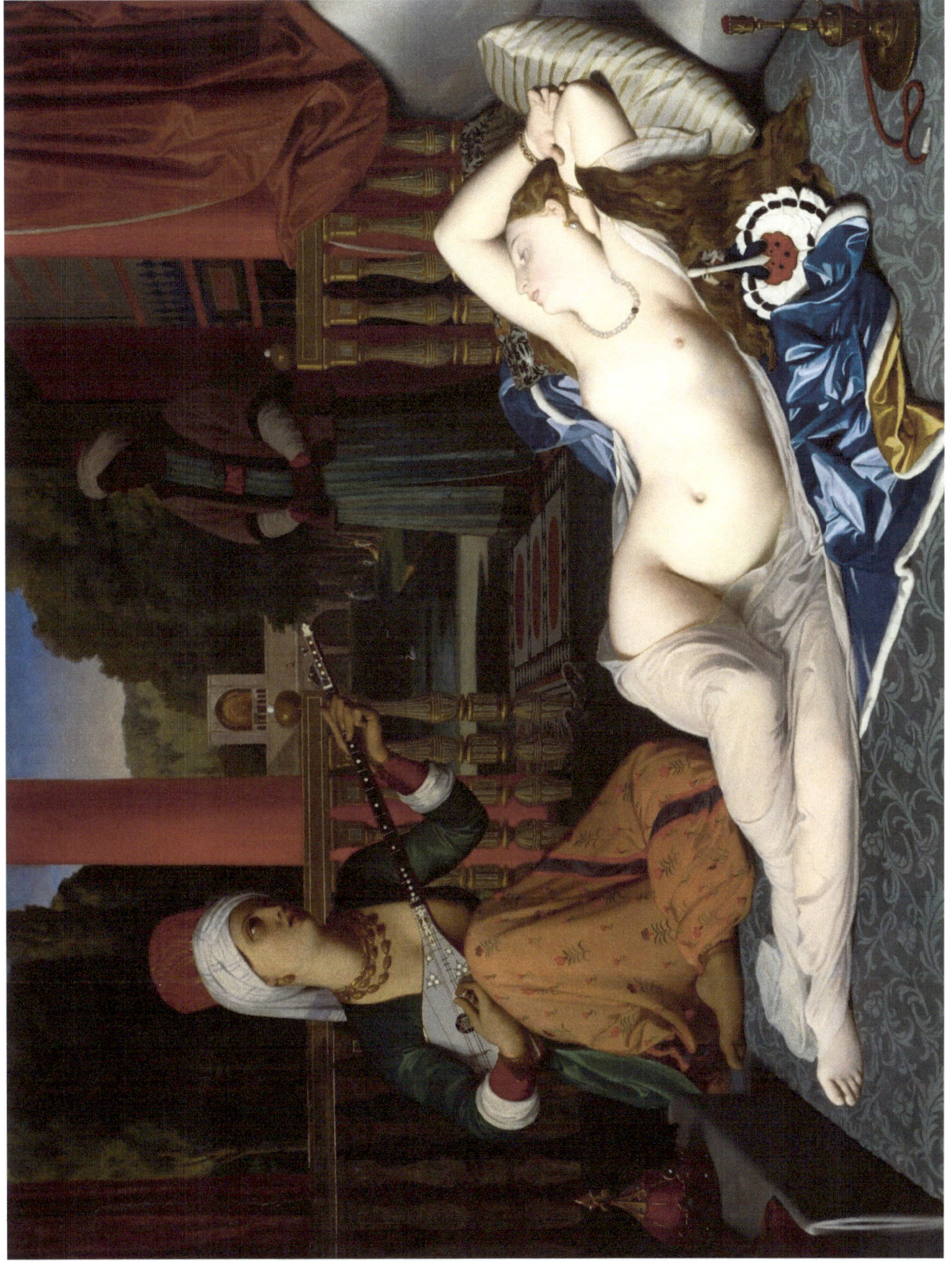

Greek Woman at Bath by Joseph-Marie Vien

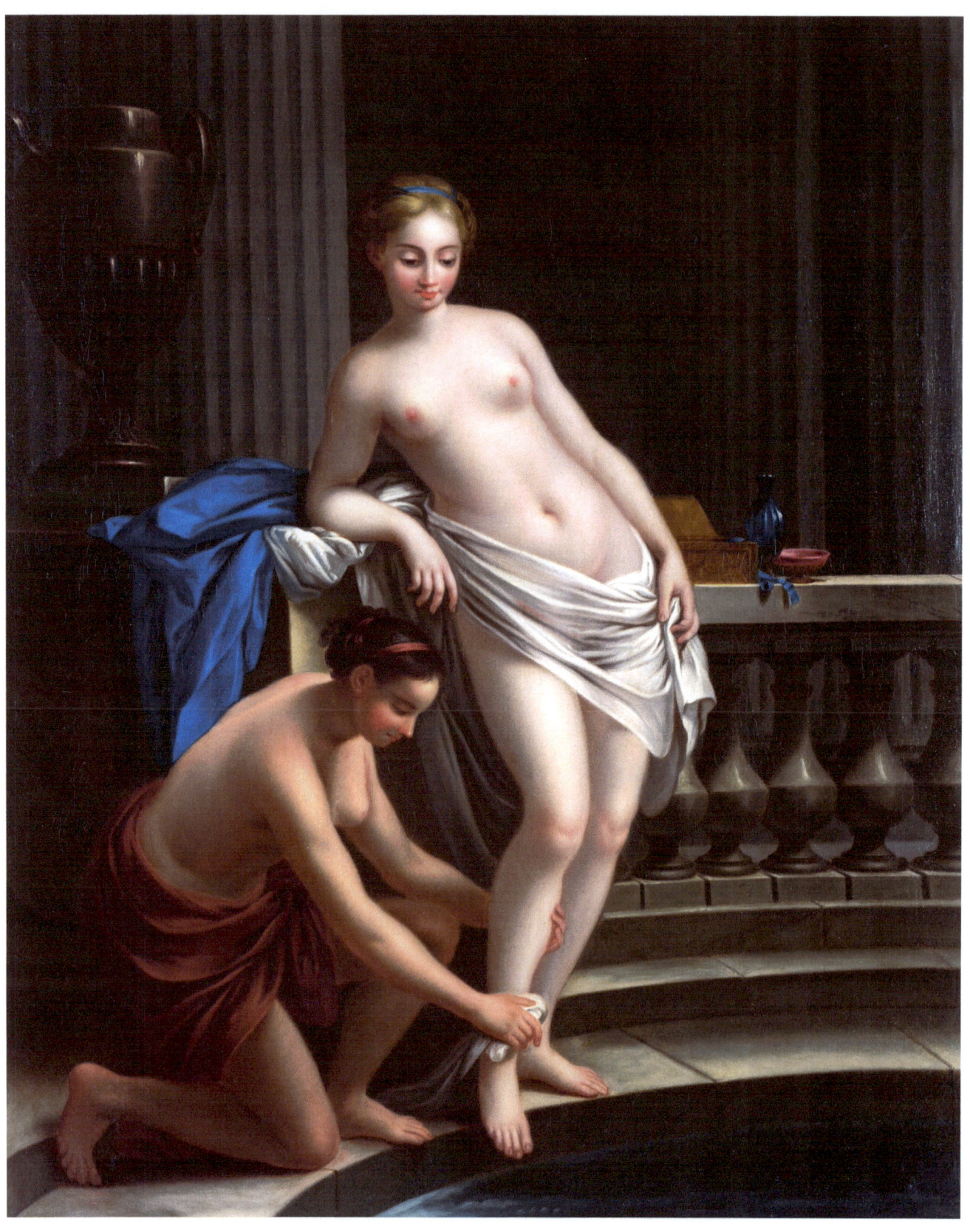

The Japanese Toilette by Marie-Francois Firmin-Girard

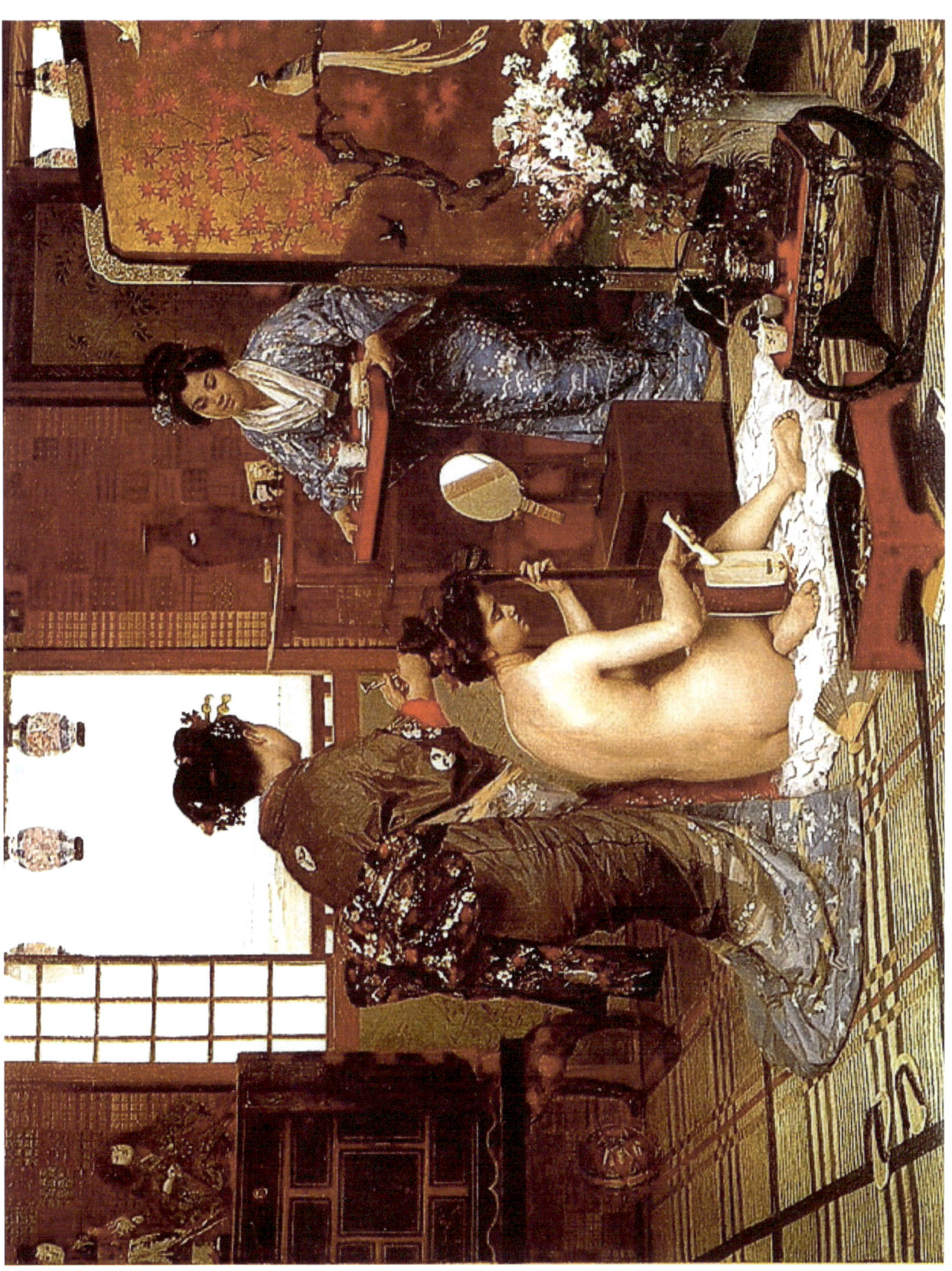

A Favorite (Roman Bath) by Sir Lawrence Alma-Tadema

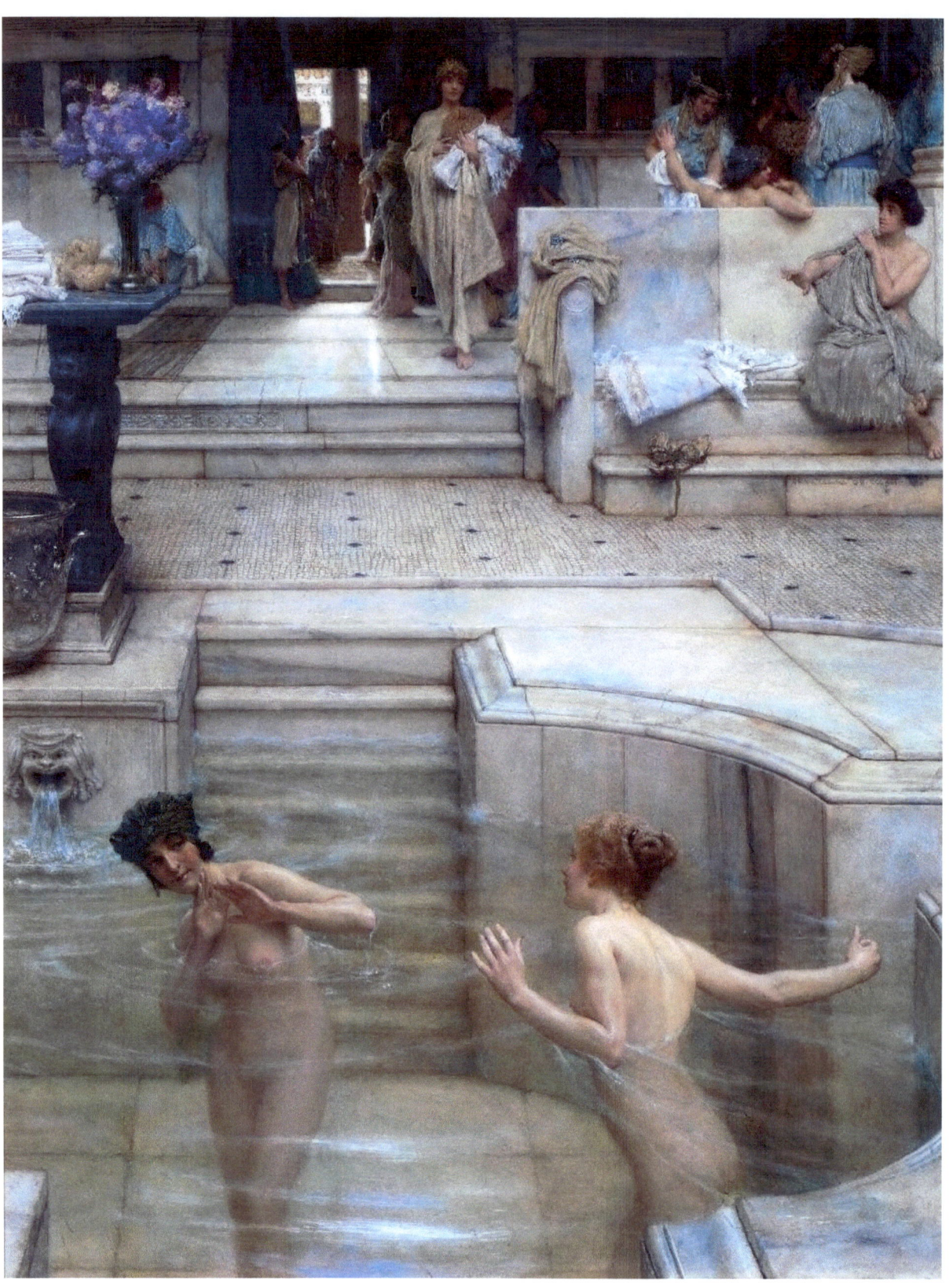

The Goddess Diana with Hunting Dog by Ferdinand Wagner

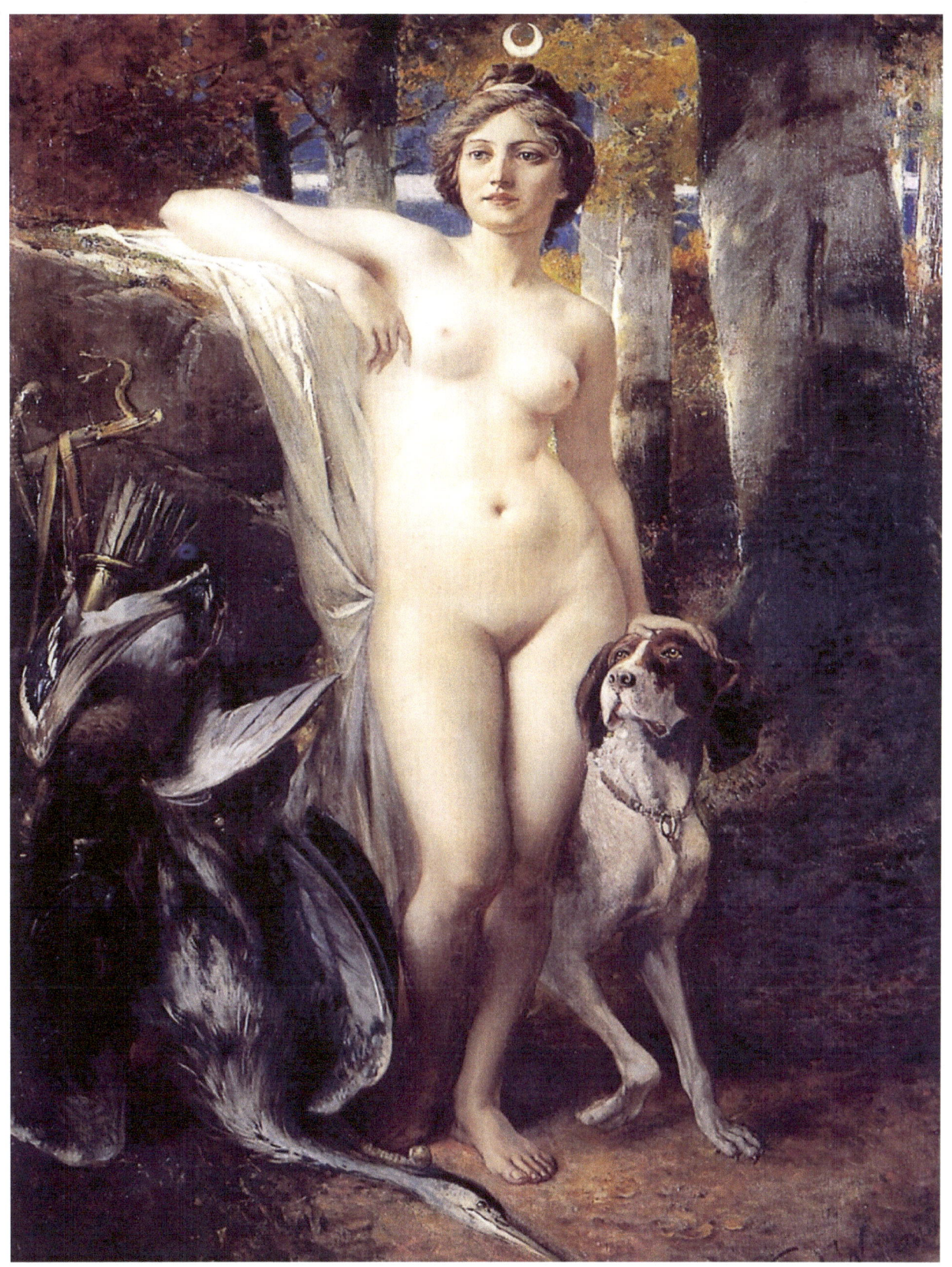

Artemis Goddess of the Hunt by Arthur Rackham

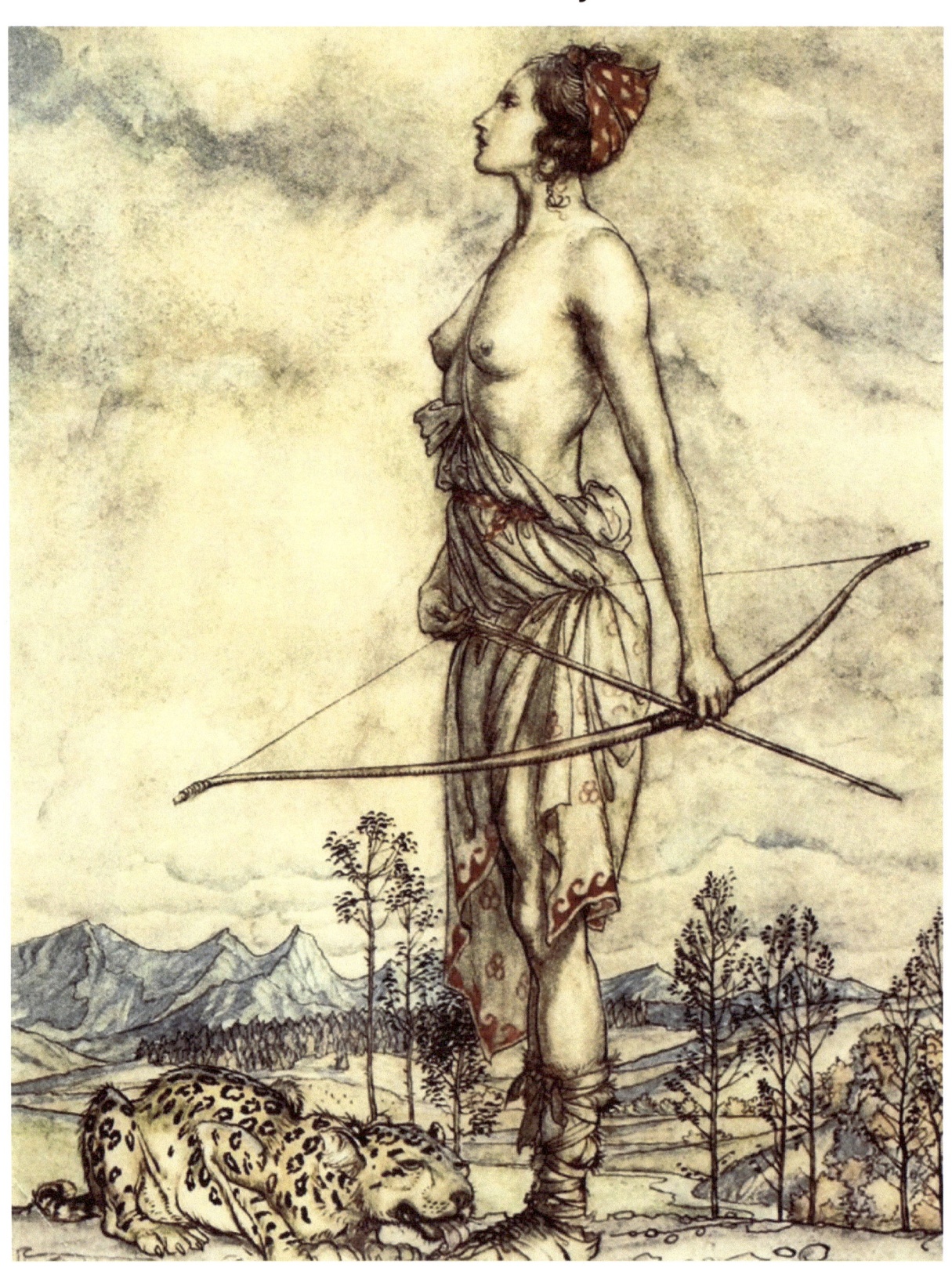

The Shipwrecked Man and the Sea by Arthur Rackham

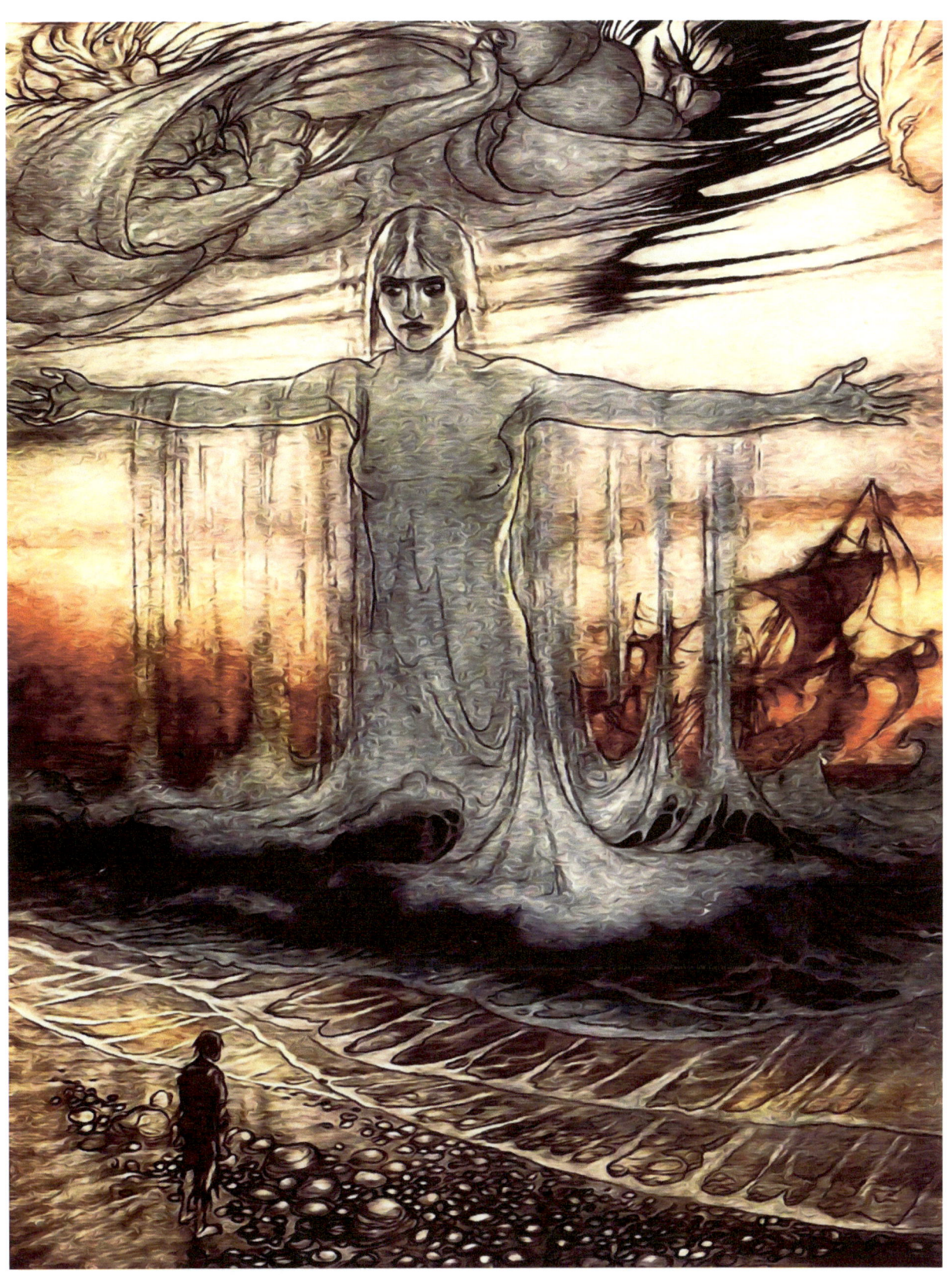

Cupid and Psyche by Jacques Louis David

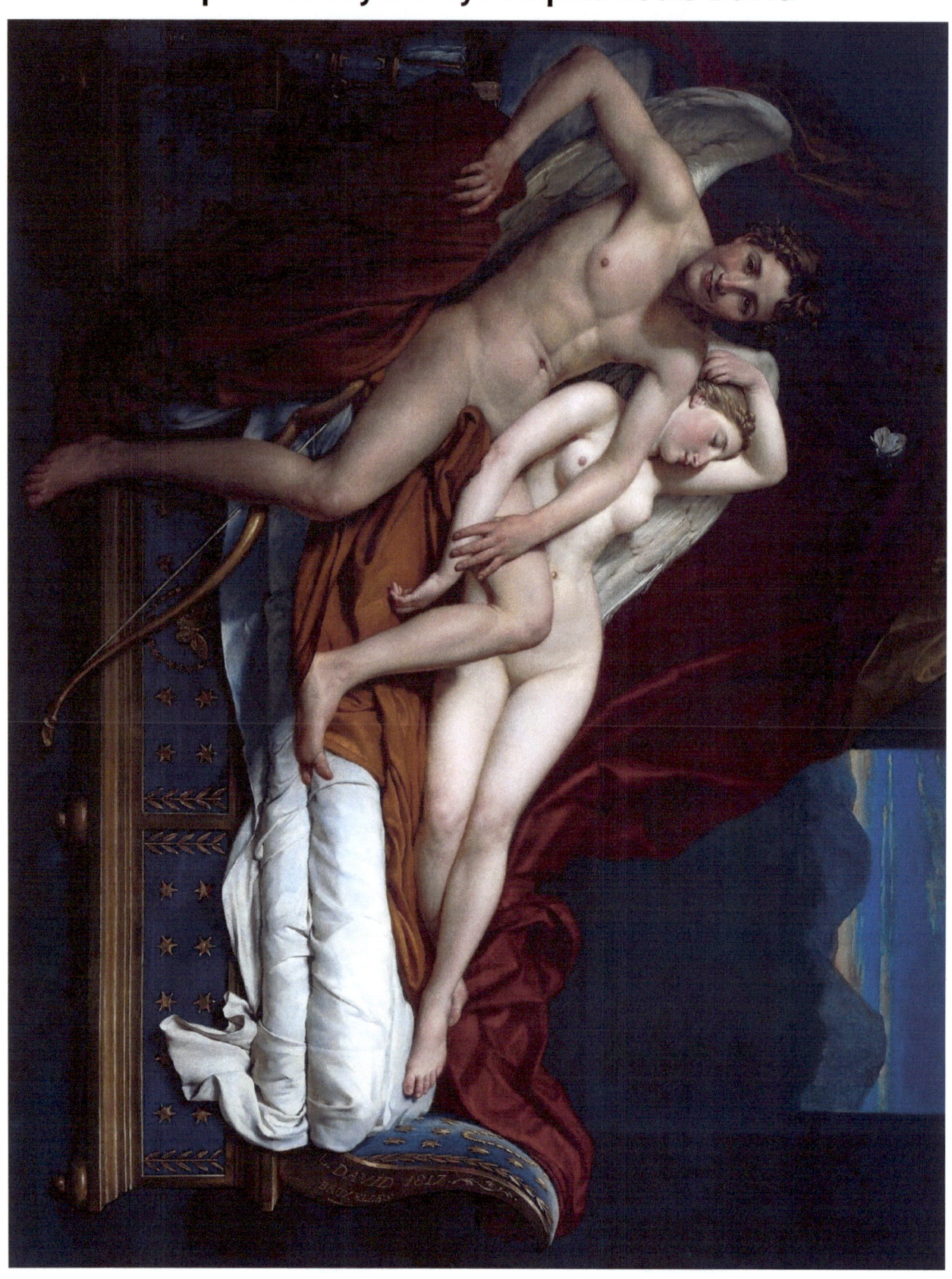

Parau na te Varua ino or Words of the Devil by Paul Gauguin

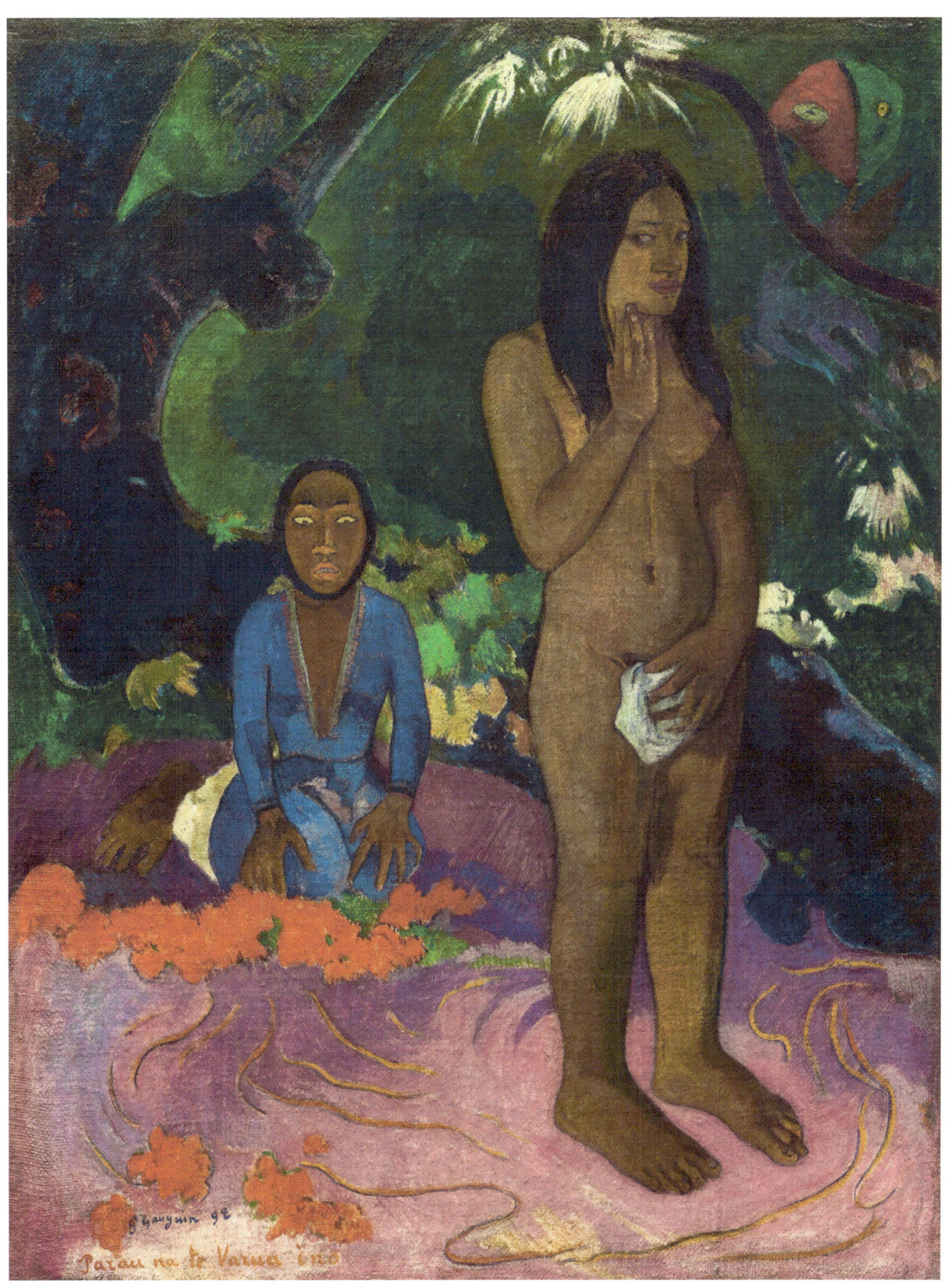

Salome, The Stomach Dance by Aubrey Beardsley

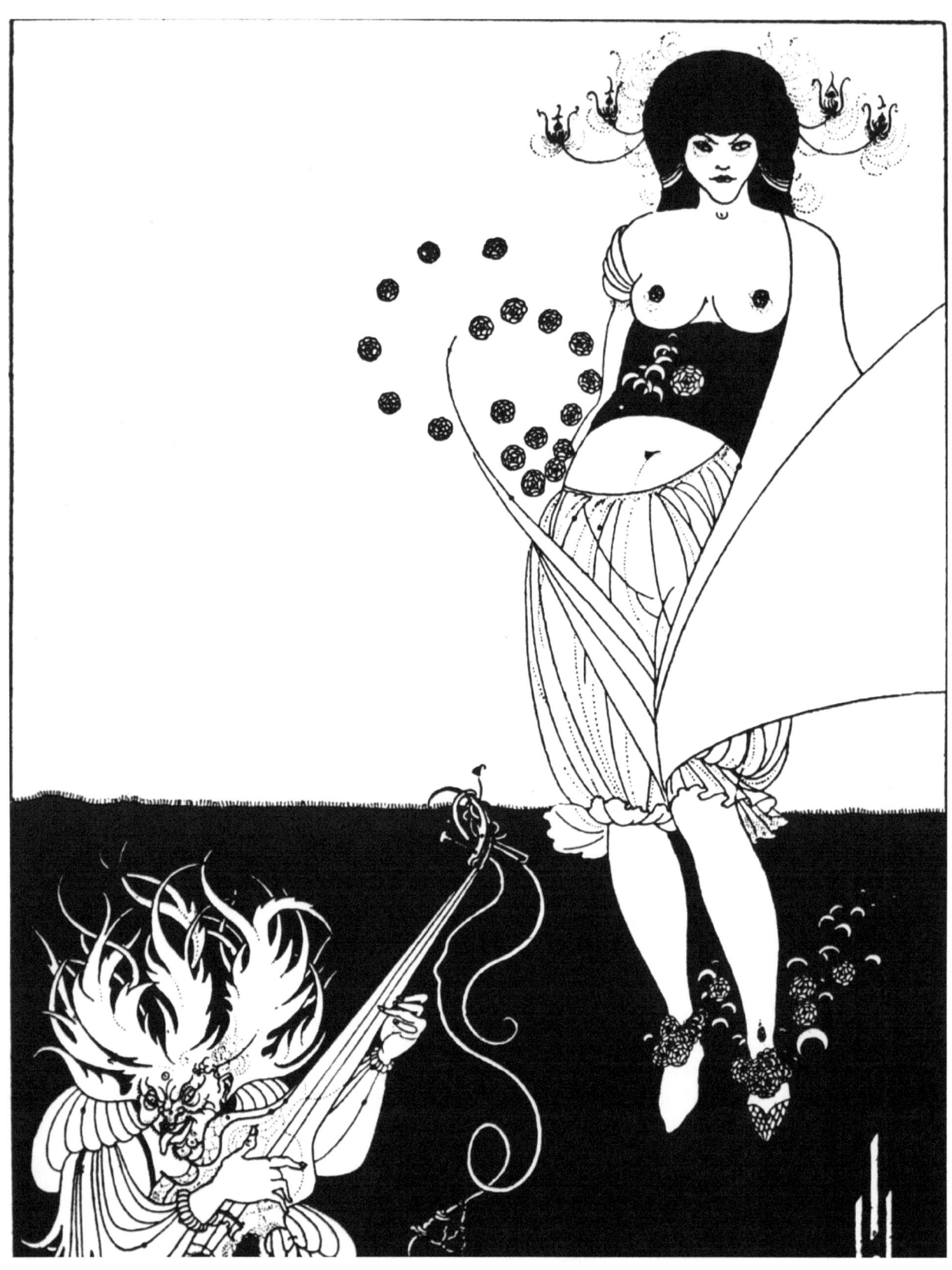

Nude Woman Reflected in Pond by Will Bradley

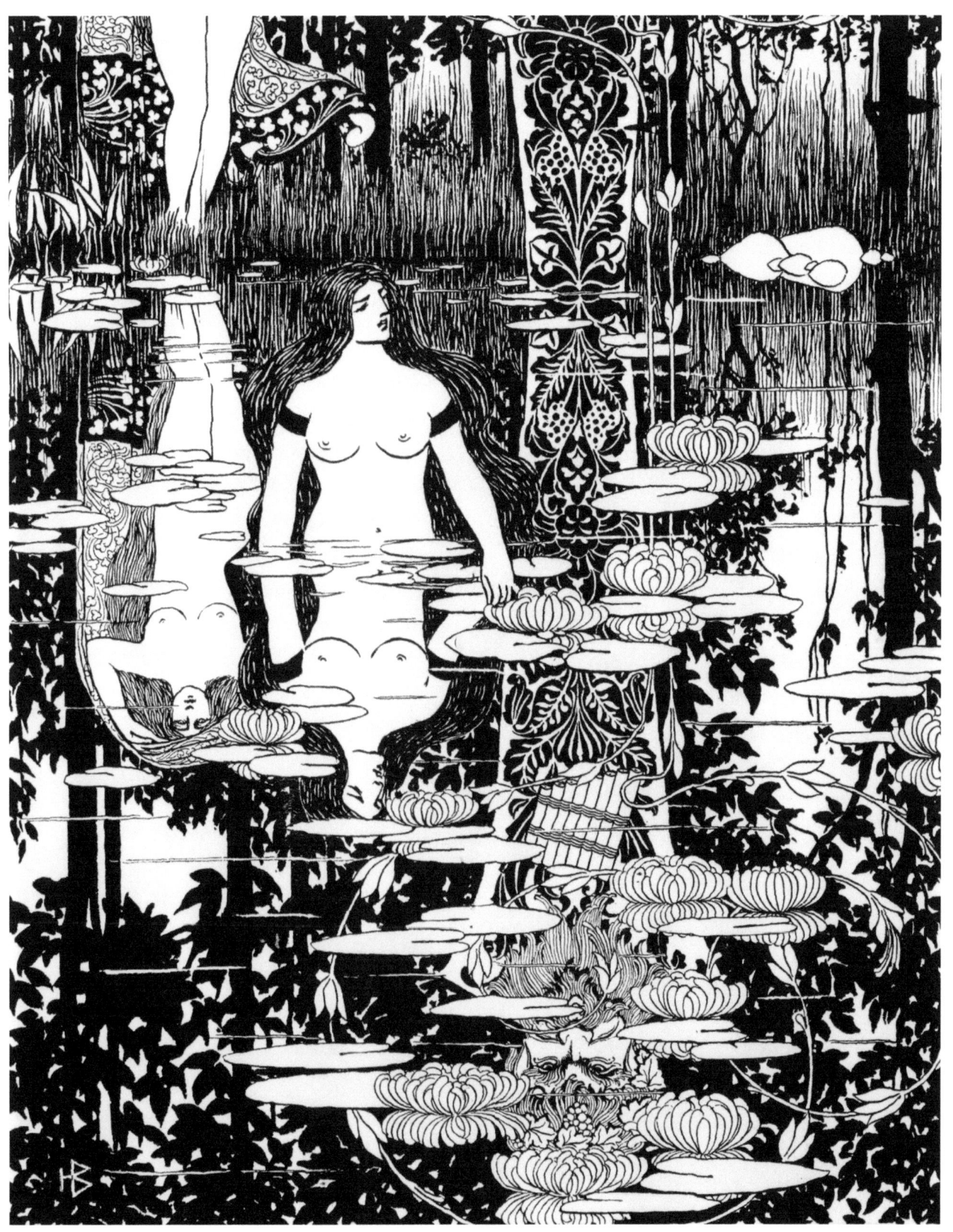

Judith by Gustav Klimt

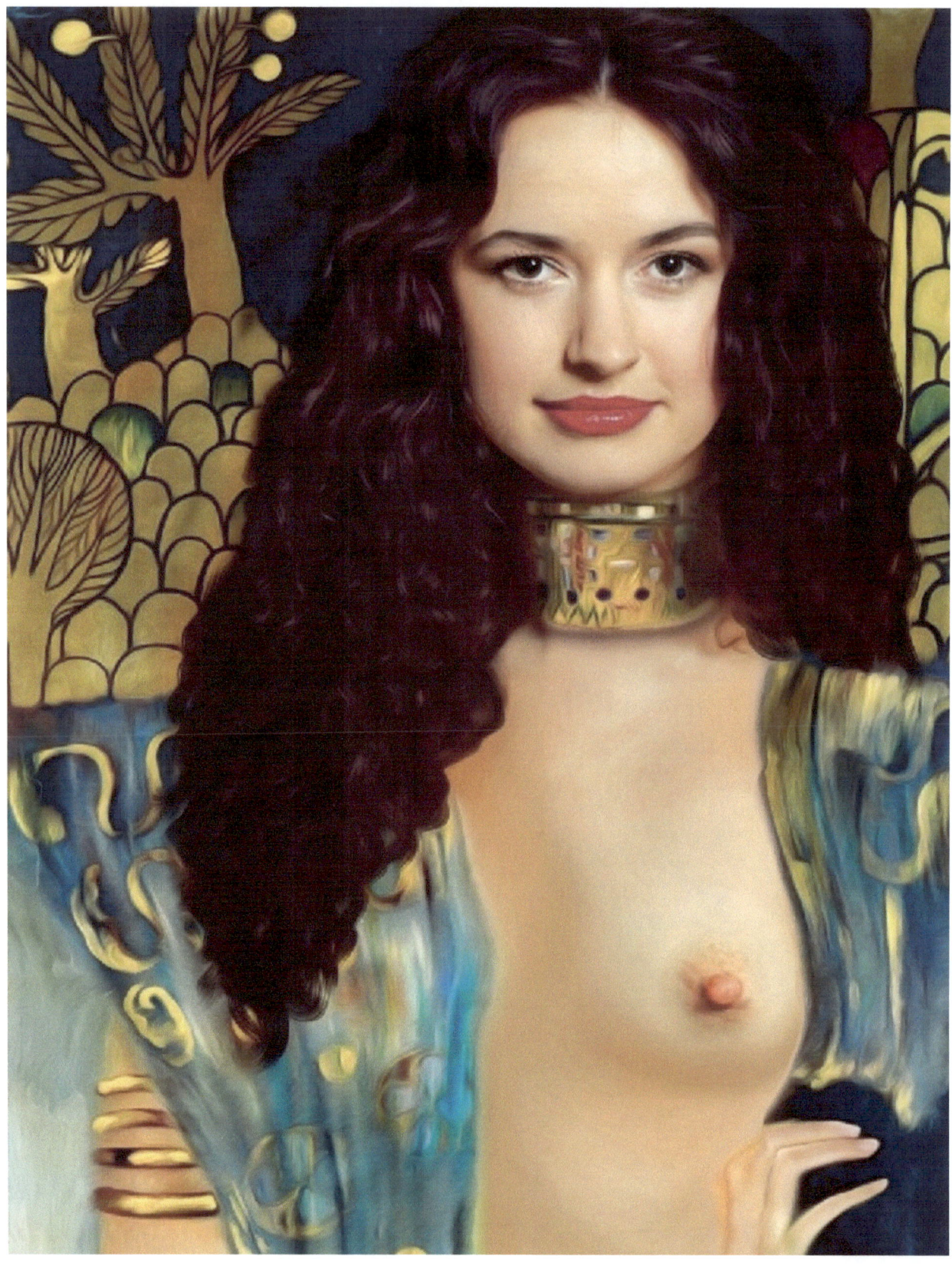

The Dancer by Gustav Klimt

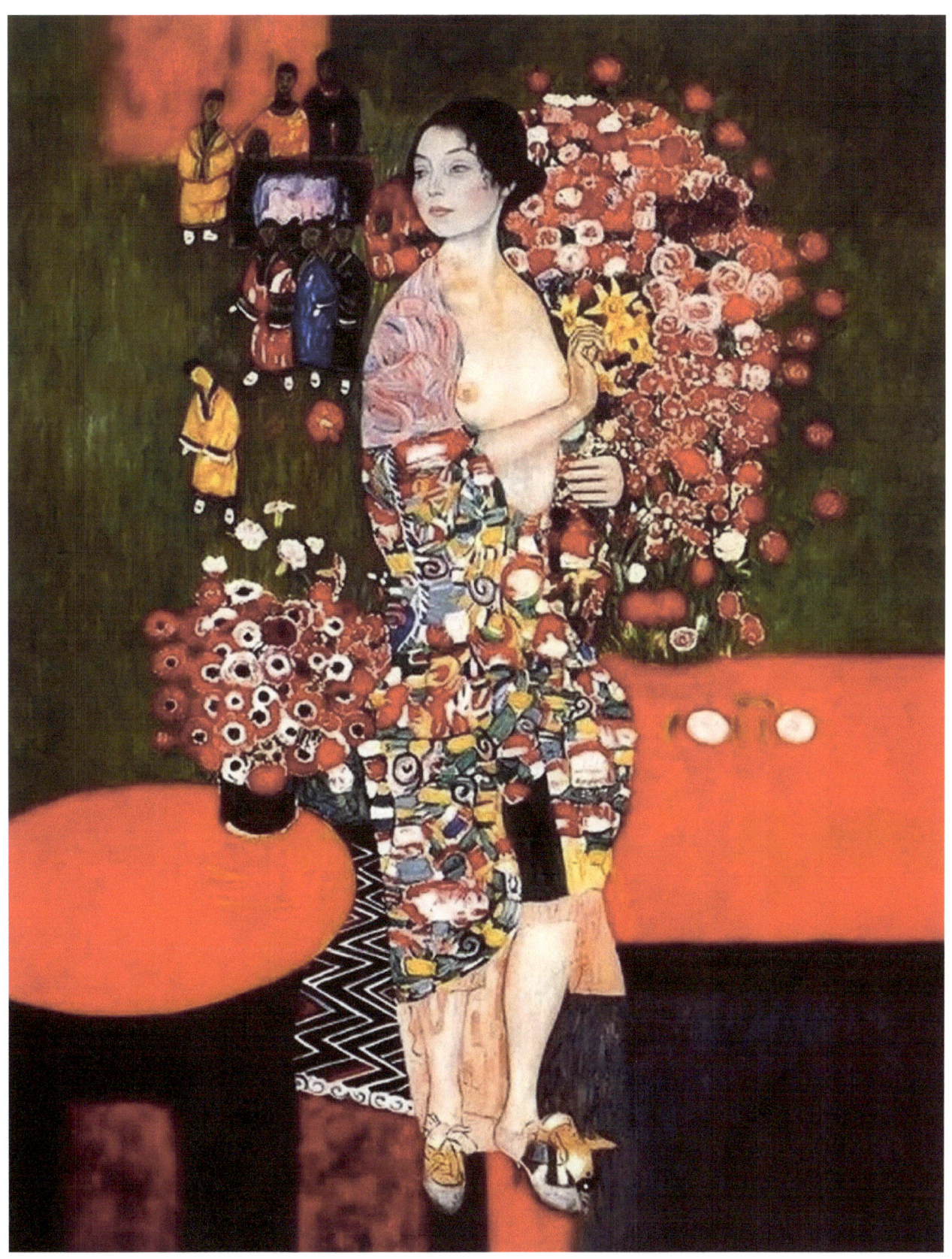

Two Friends by Gustav Klimt

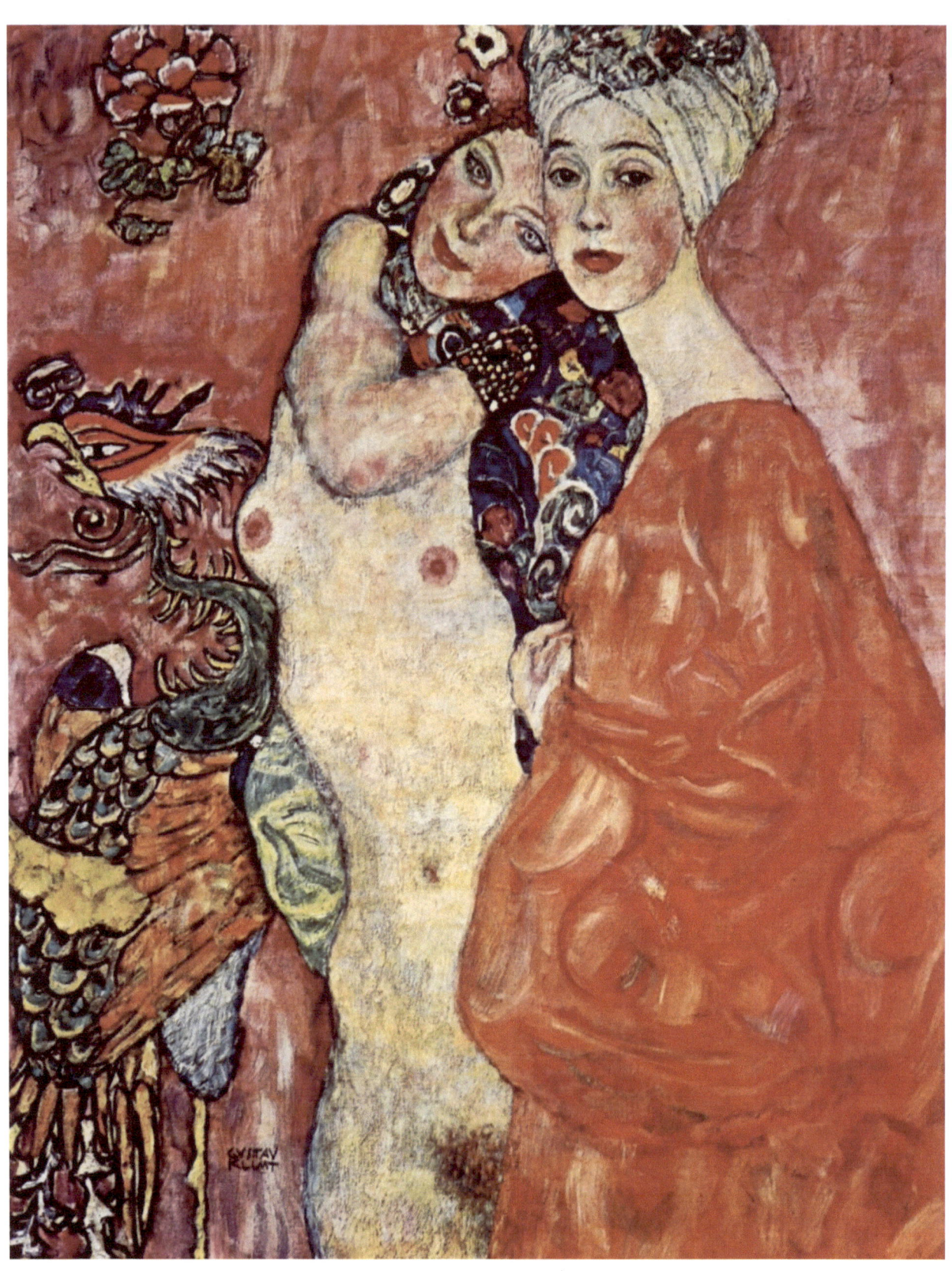

Eve and Adam by Gustav Klimt

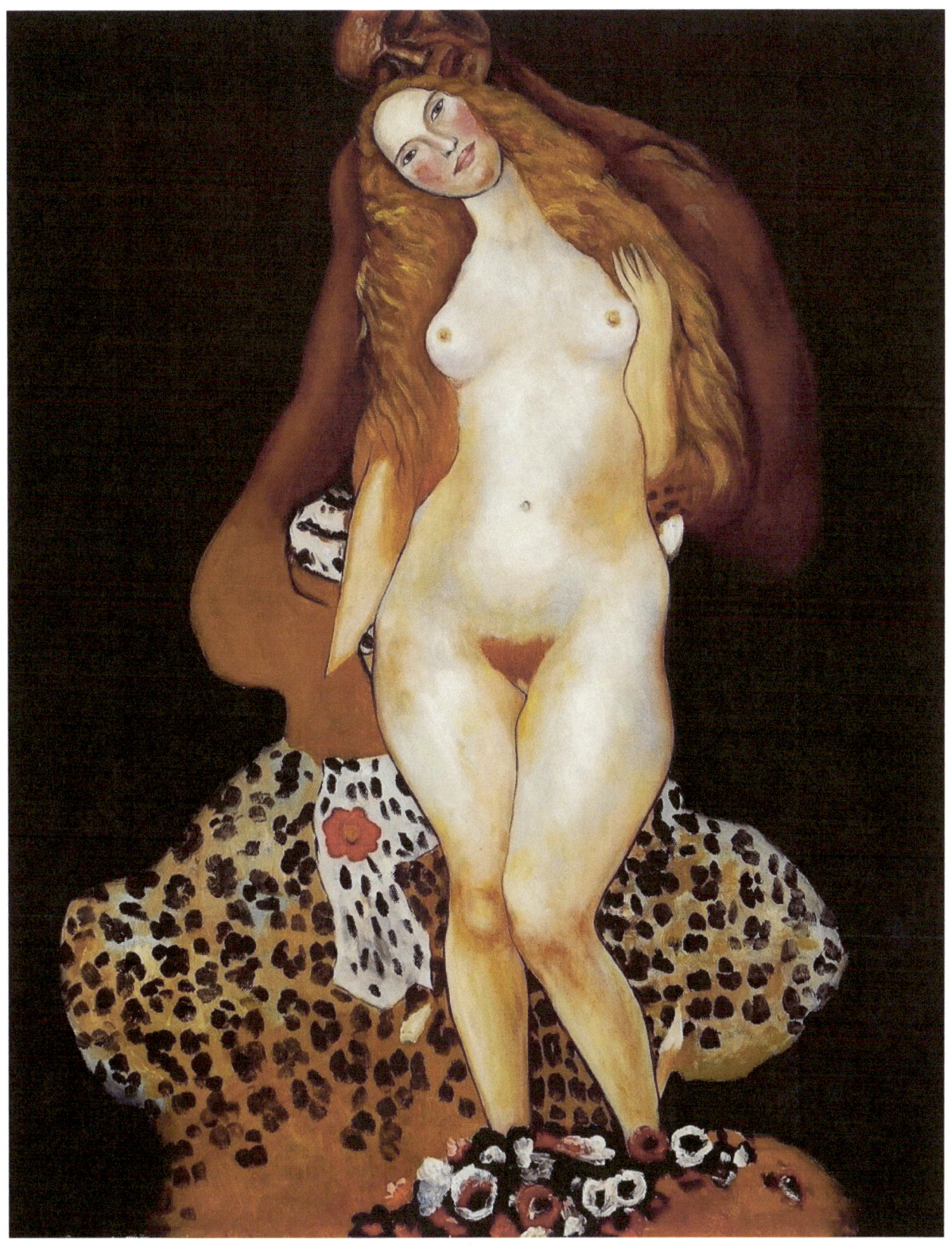

Psyche and Pan by Ernst Klimt

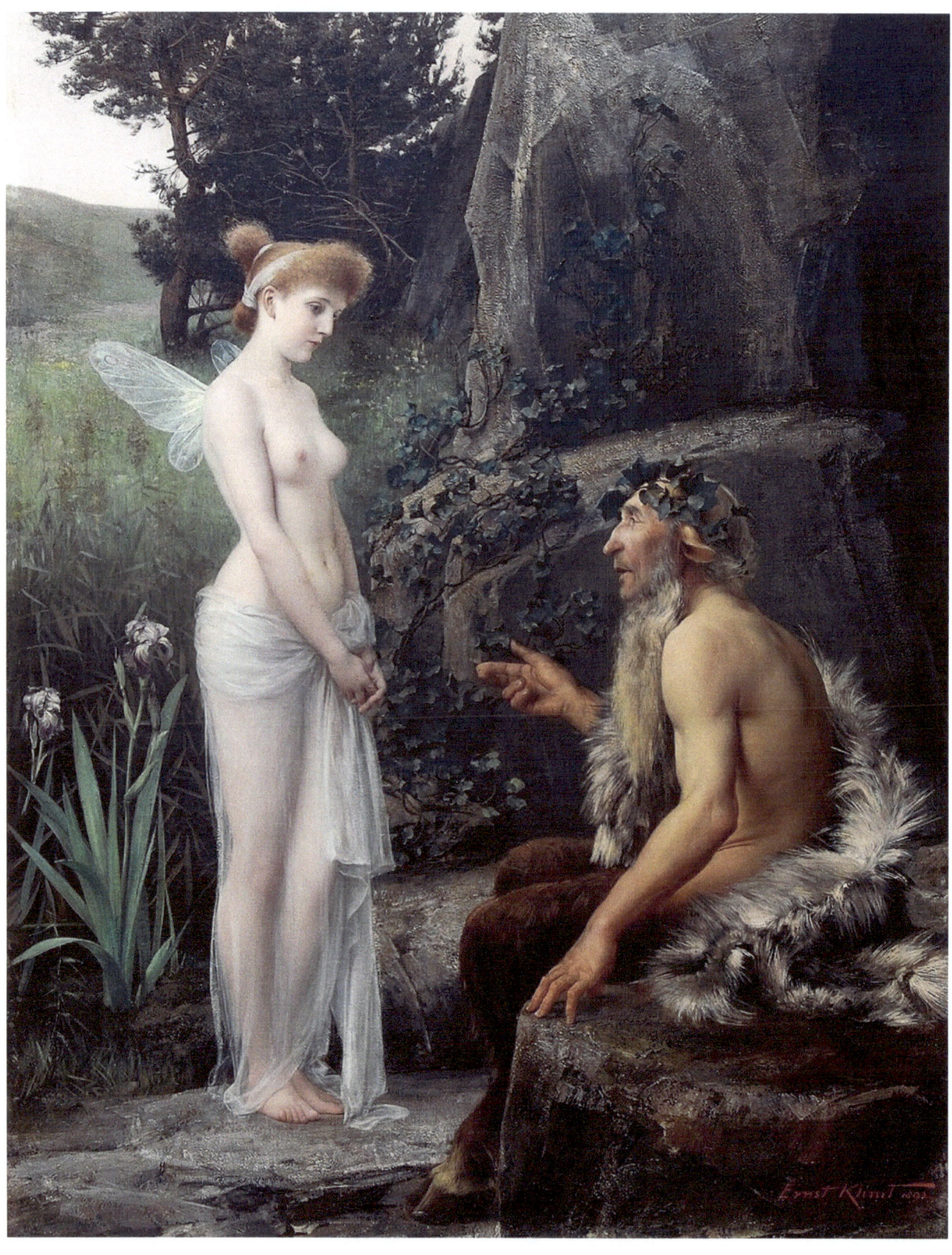

Nude Woman with Chestnut Hair by Angelo Asti

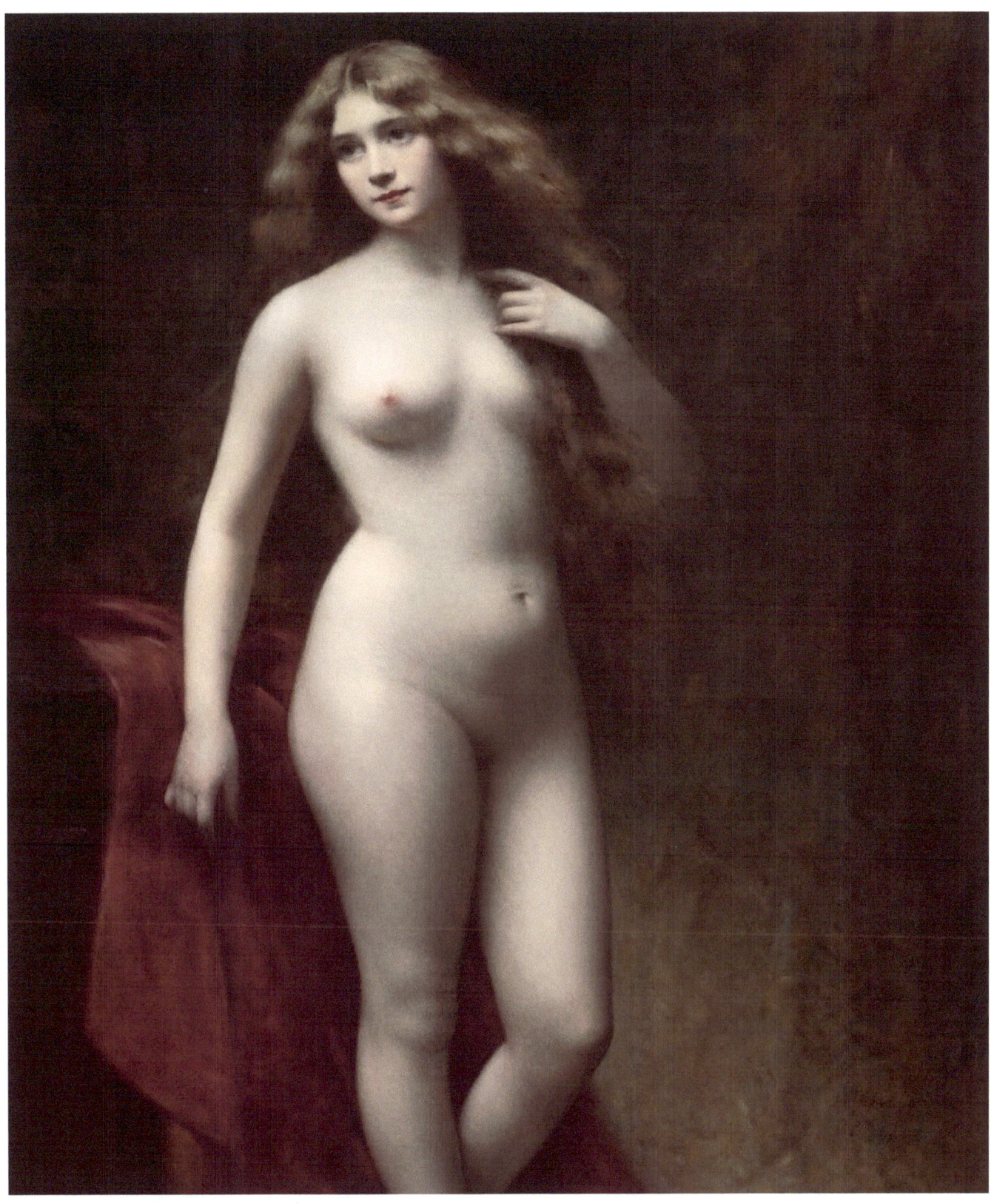

Nude Woman In Werner's Rowing Boat by Anders Zorn

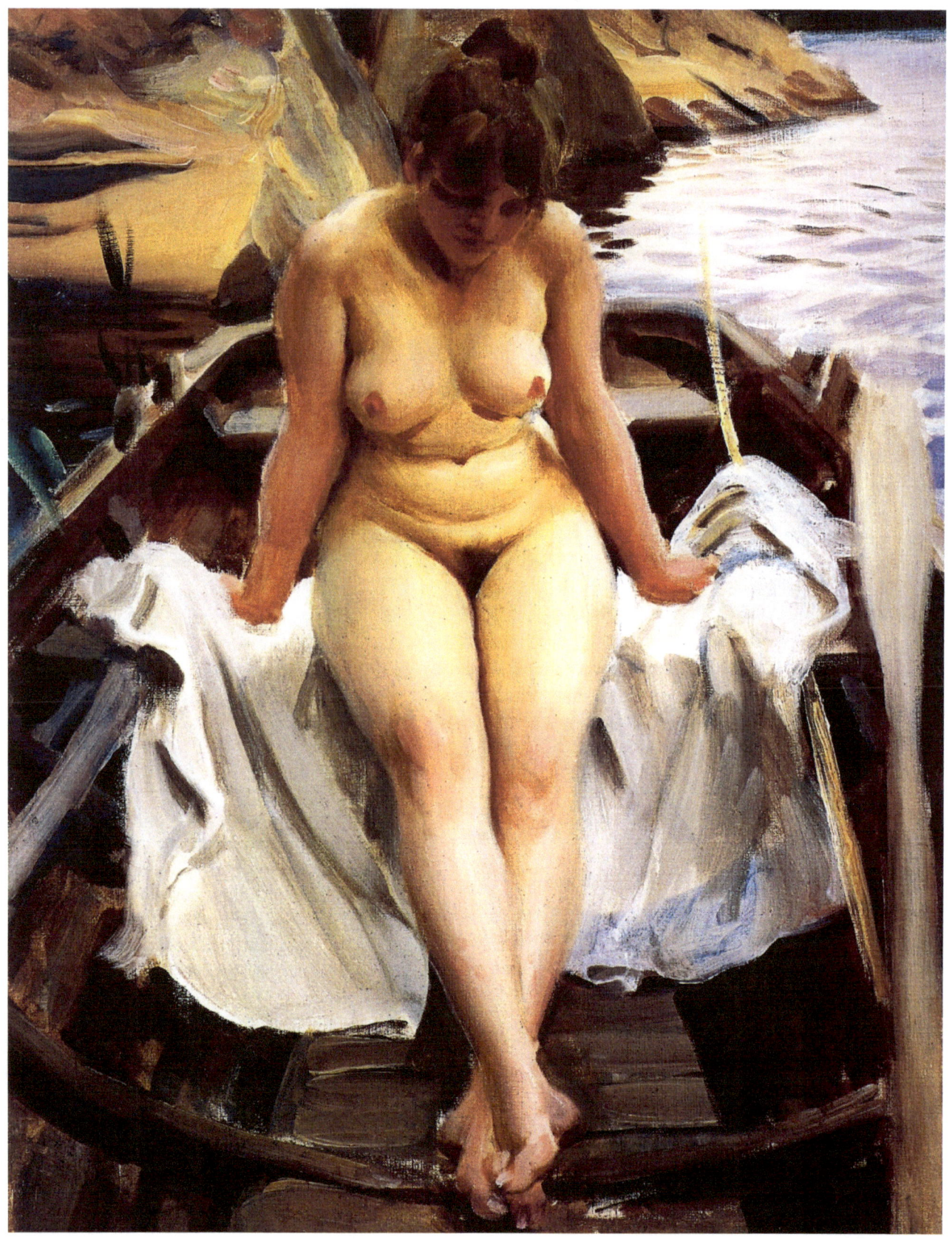

The Young Bather by Victor Tortez

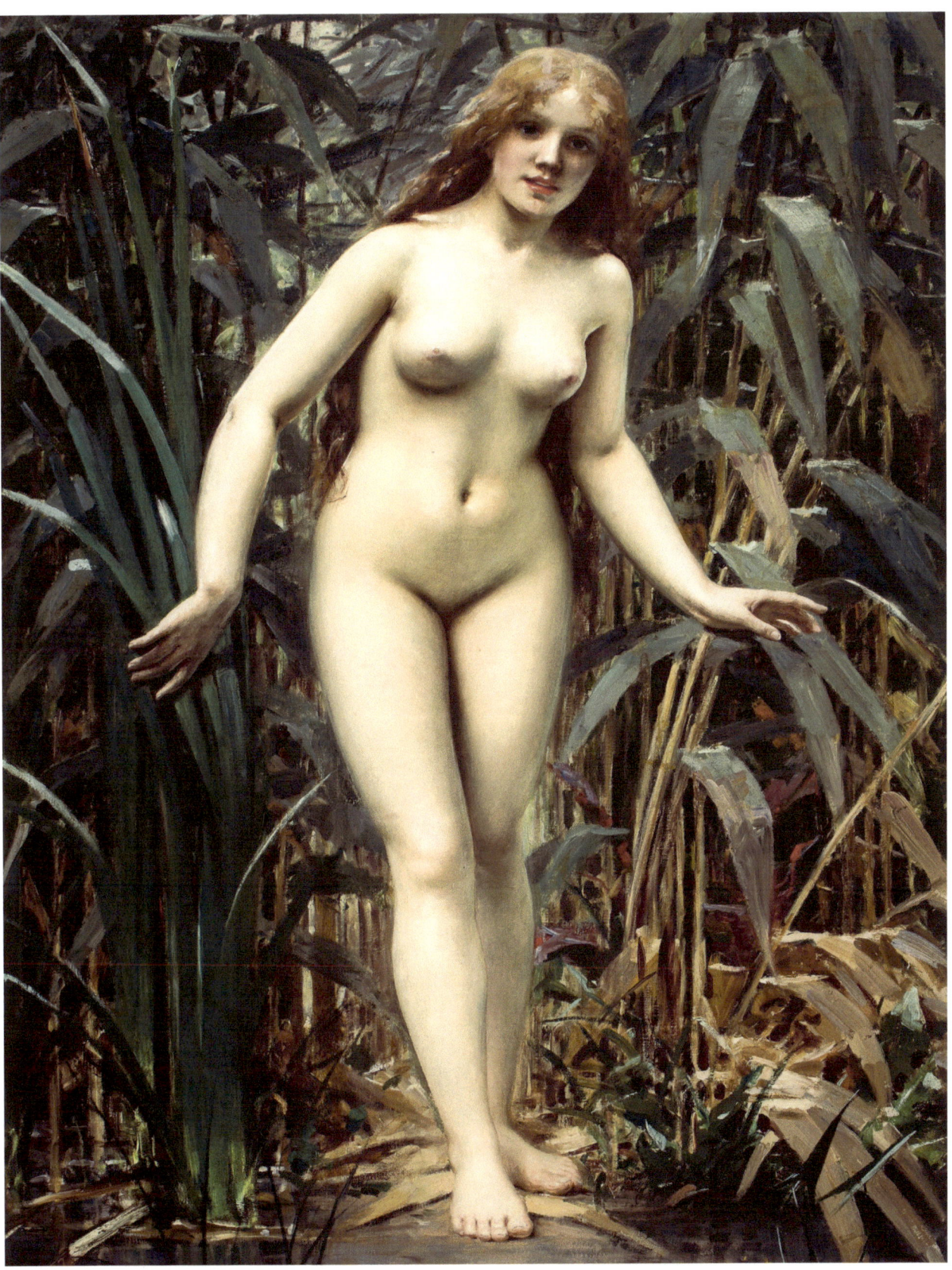

Nude Princess of India by Richard Borrmeister

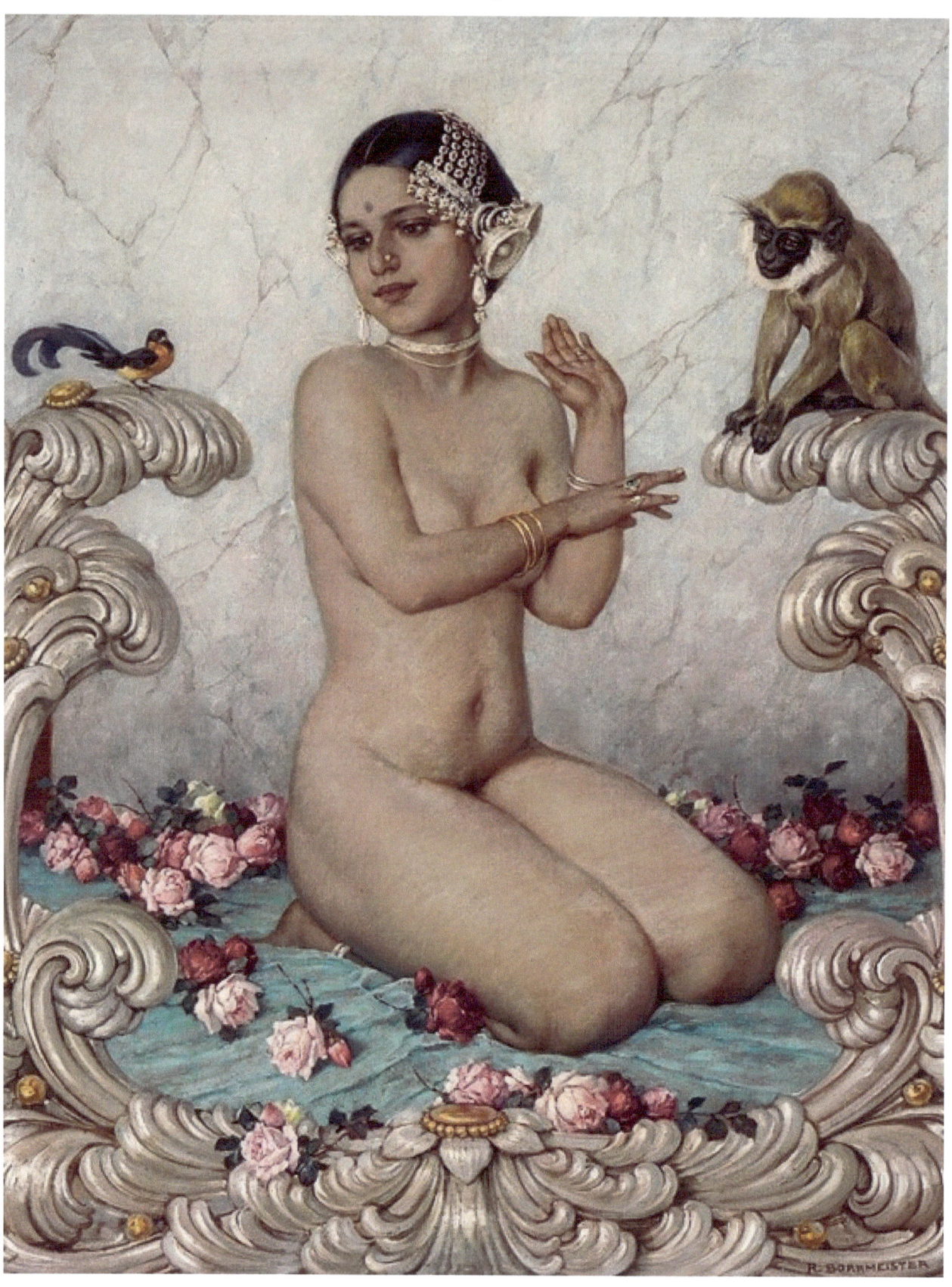

Love Nymph by Anders Zorn

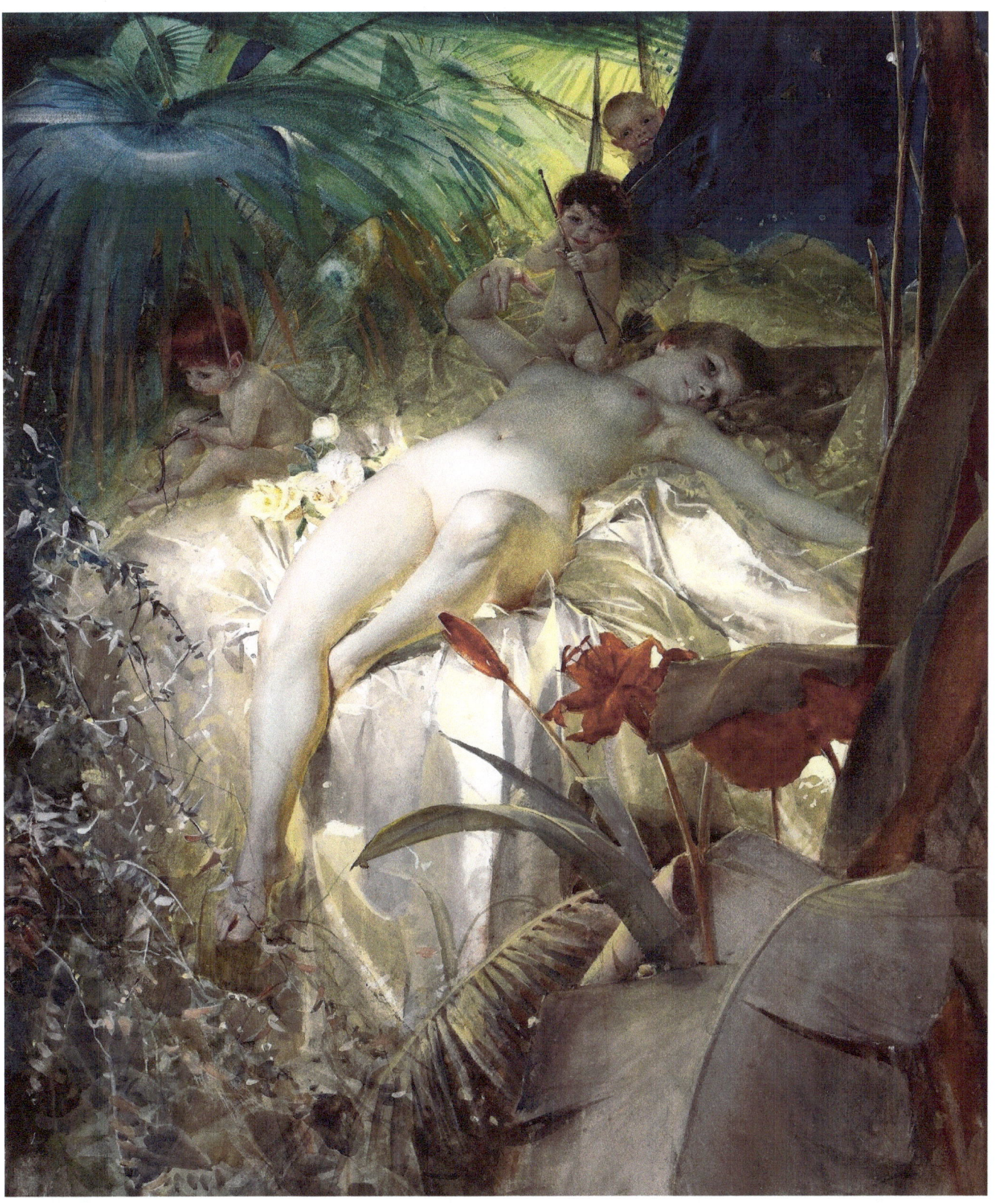

Madonna by Edvard Munch

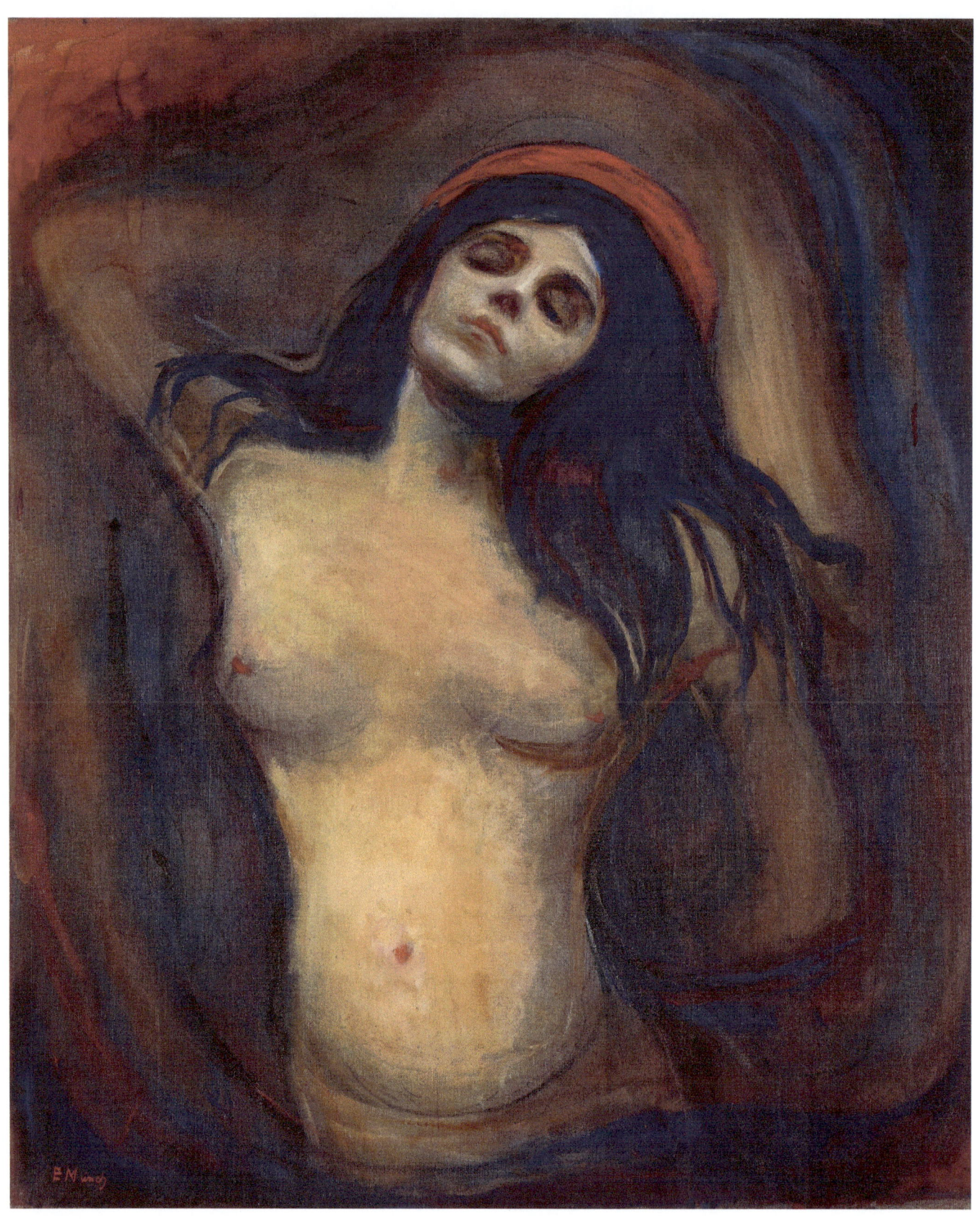

A Seated Female by Girolamo Siciolante da Sermoneta

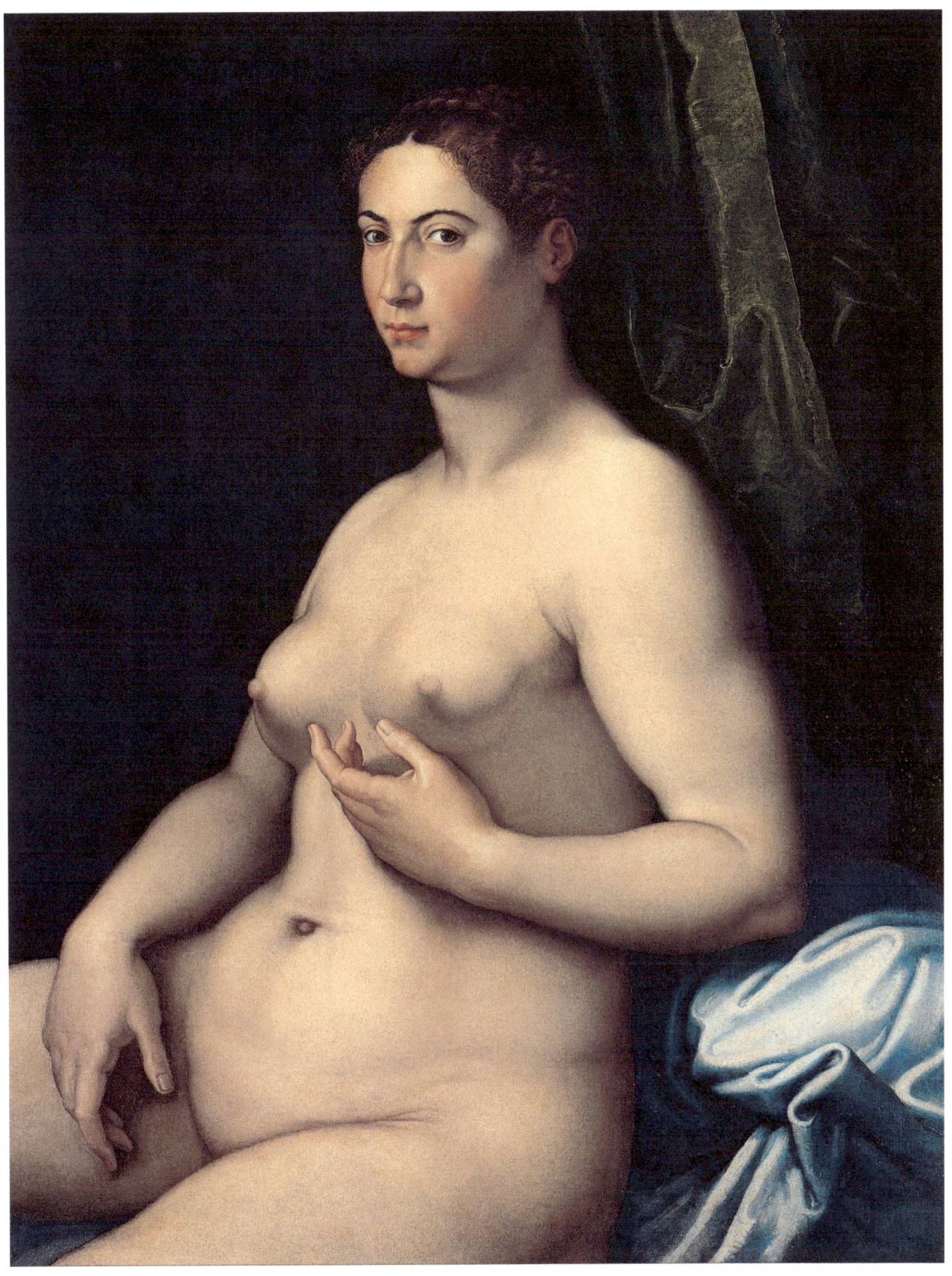

Nude Asleep on Bed by Henri Lebasque

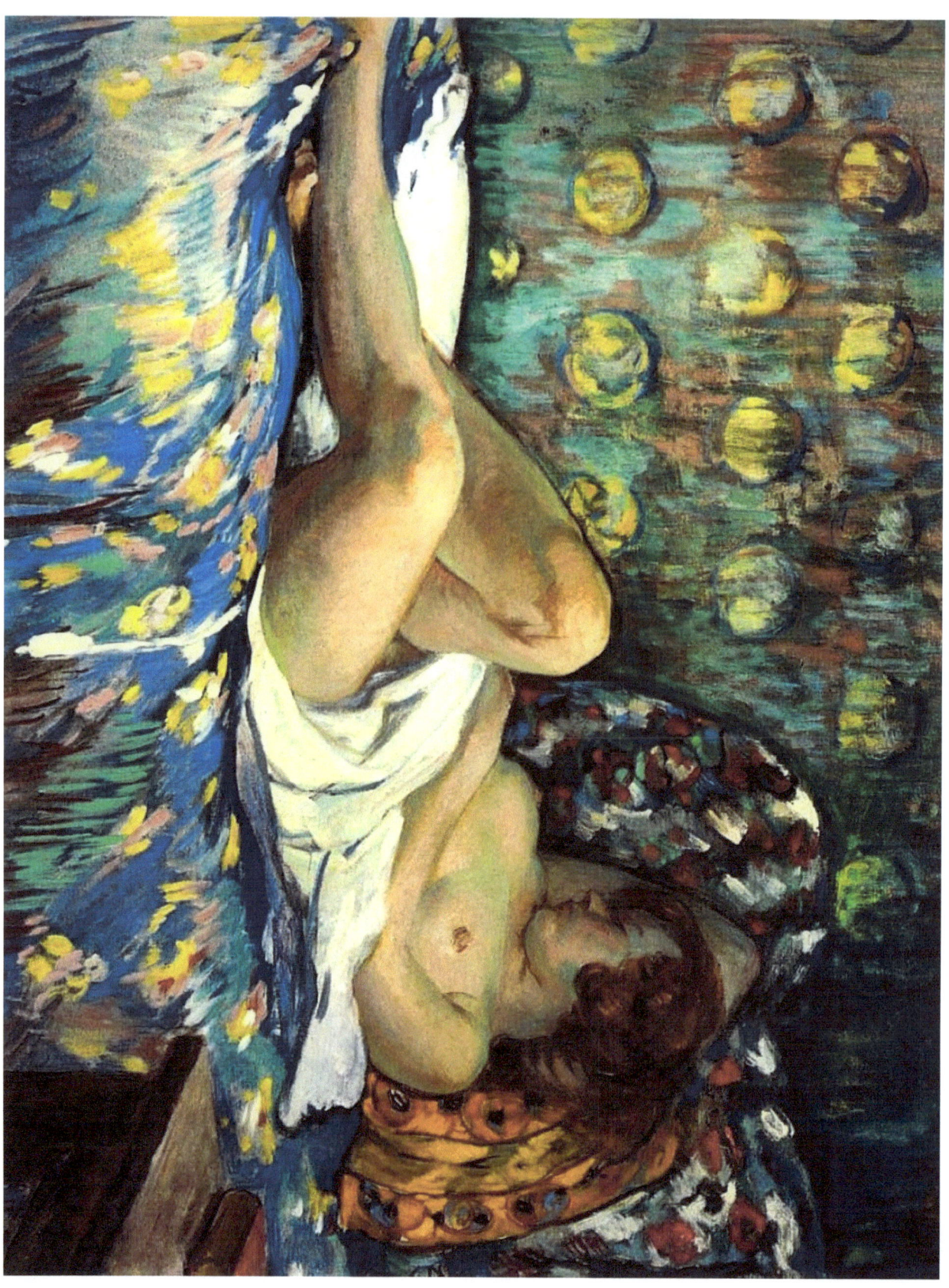

Nude Sitting on Edge of Bed by Henri Lebasque

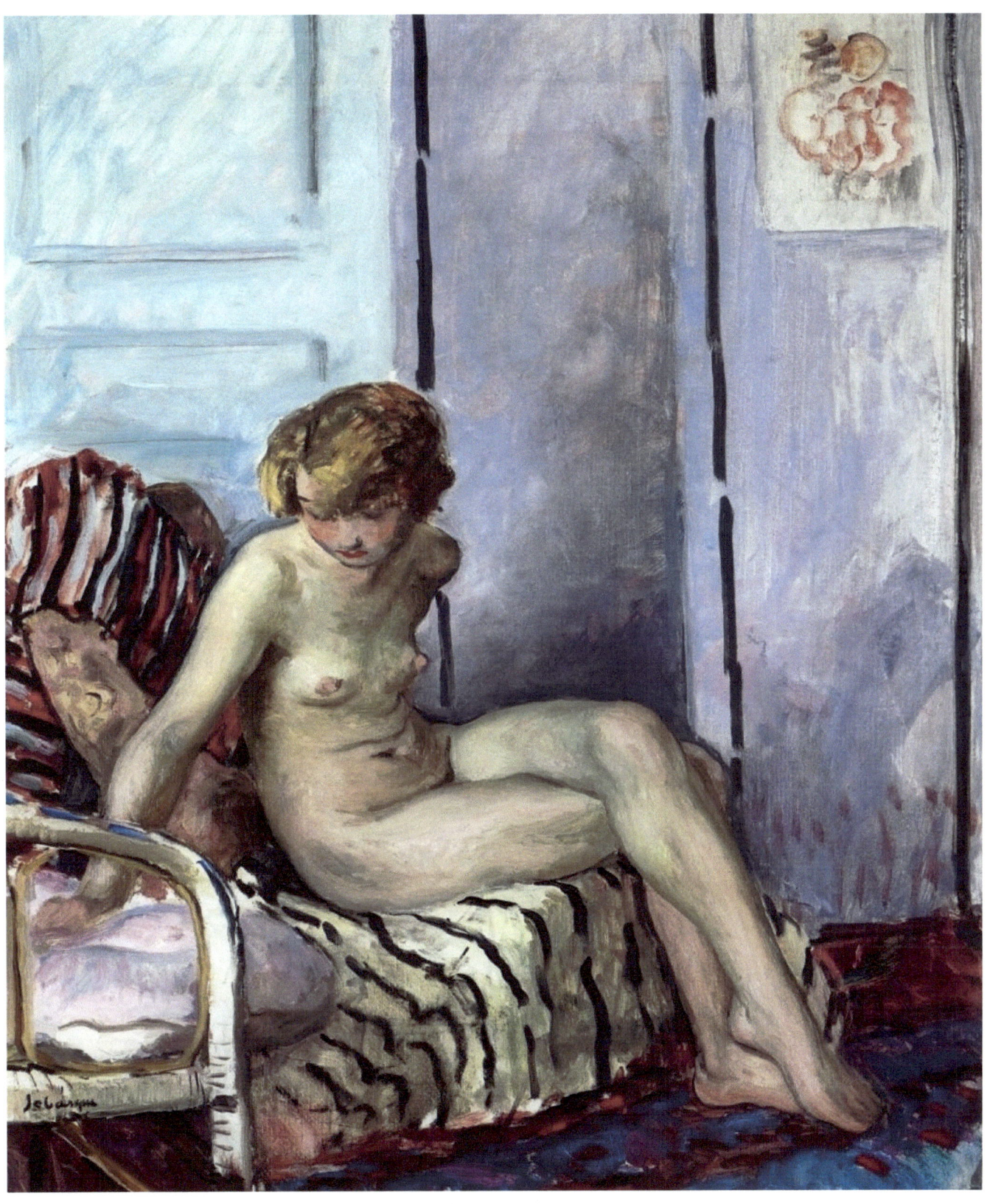

Nude Woman Seated at Dressing Table by Frederick Carl Frieseke

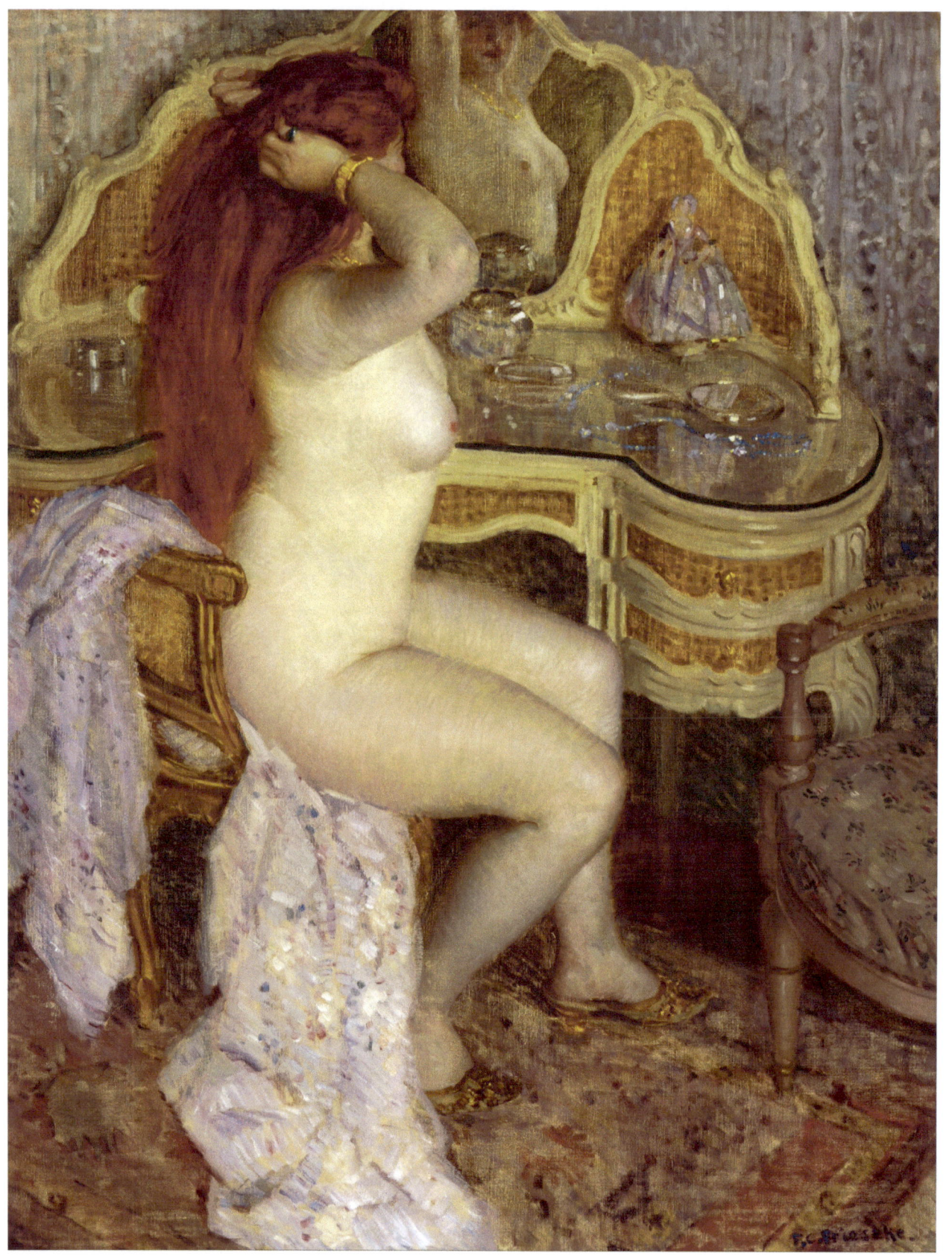

Nude Girl by Lovis Corinth

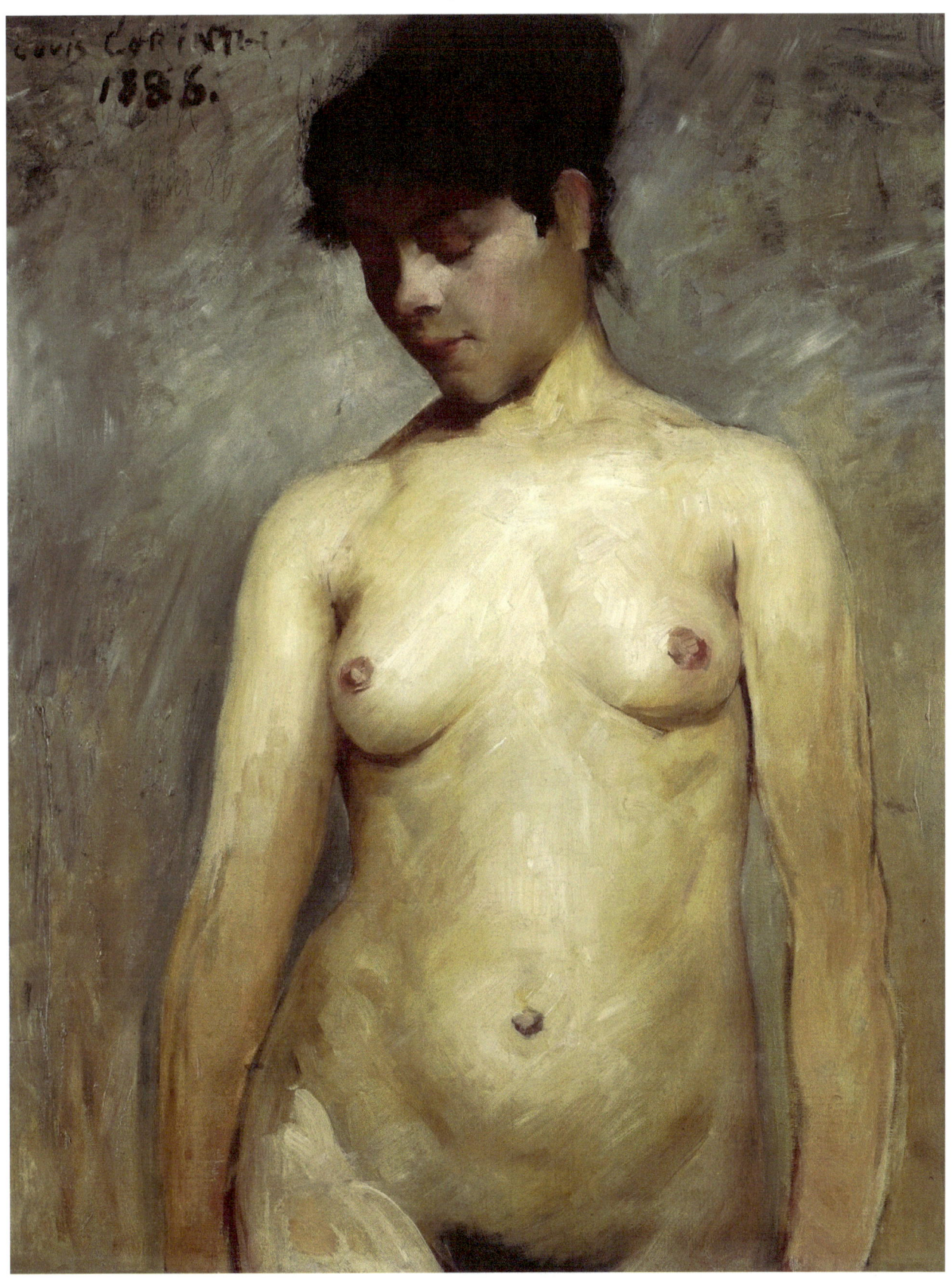

The Turkish Bath by Felix Edouard Vallotton

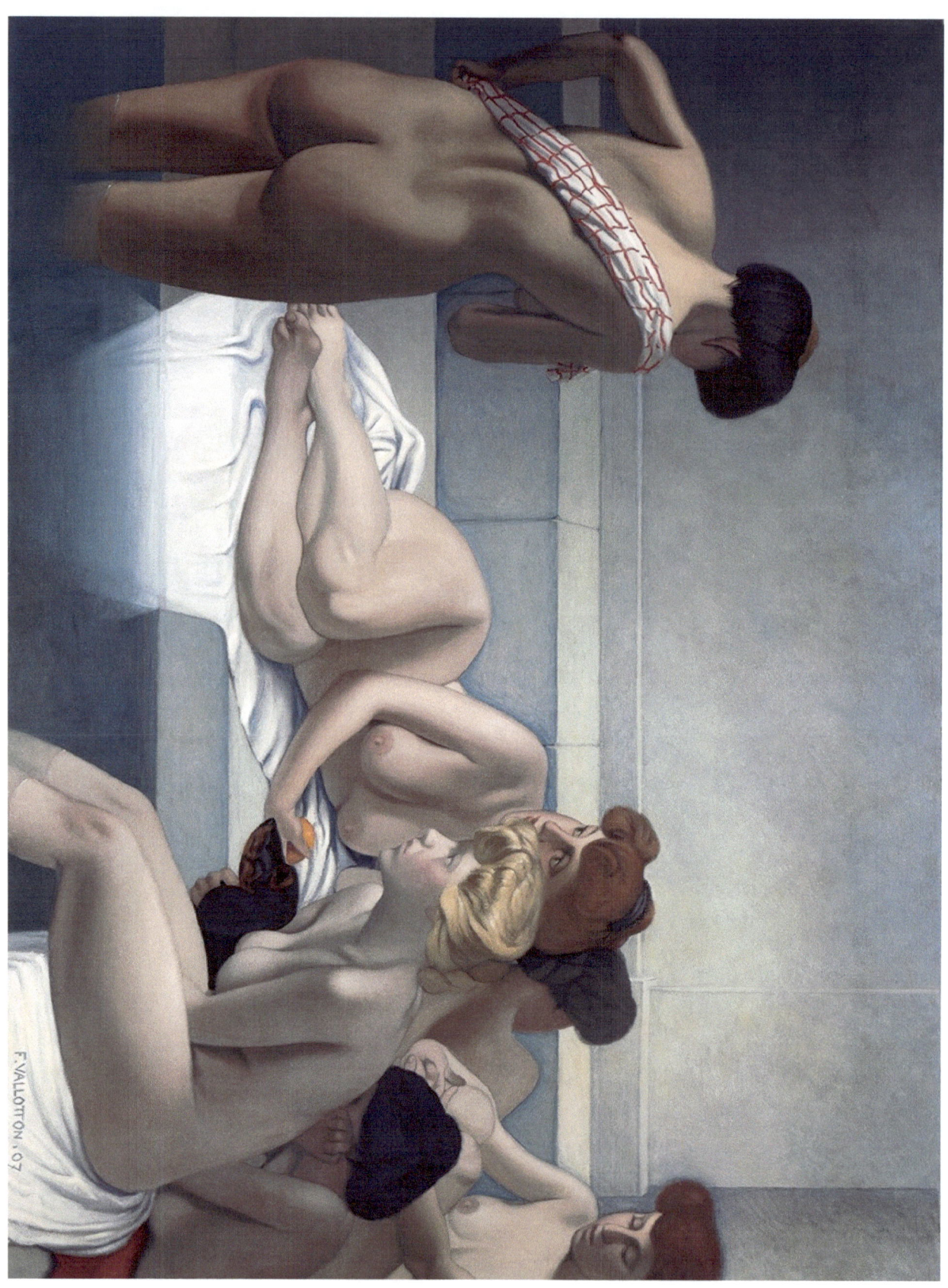

Nude Pregnant Woman with Shadow by Ismael Nery

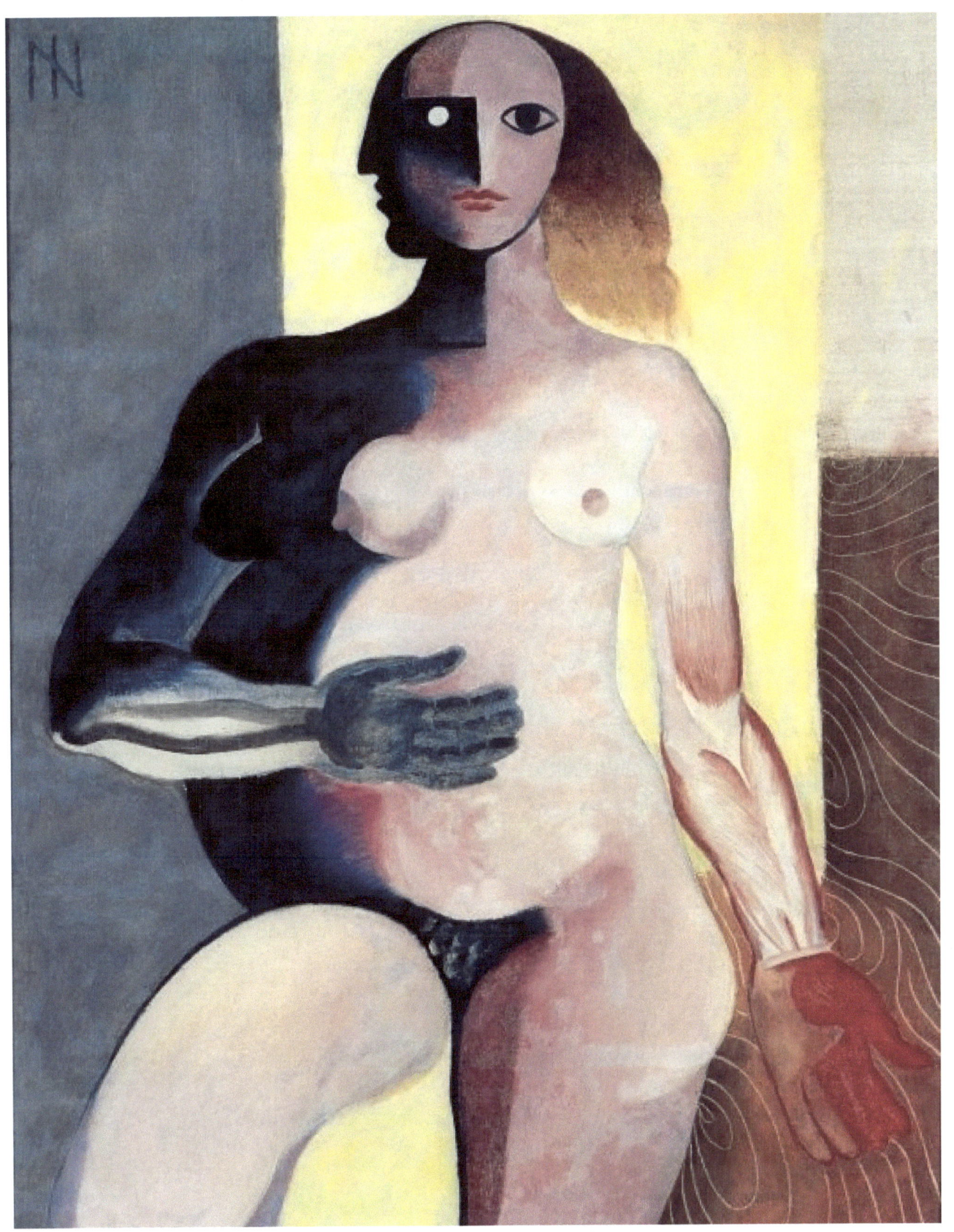

Nude Woman Sitting with Flowers by Ismael Nery

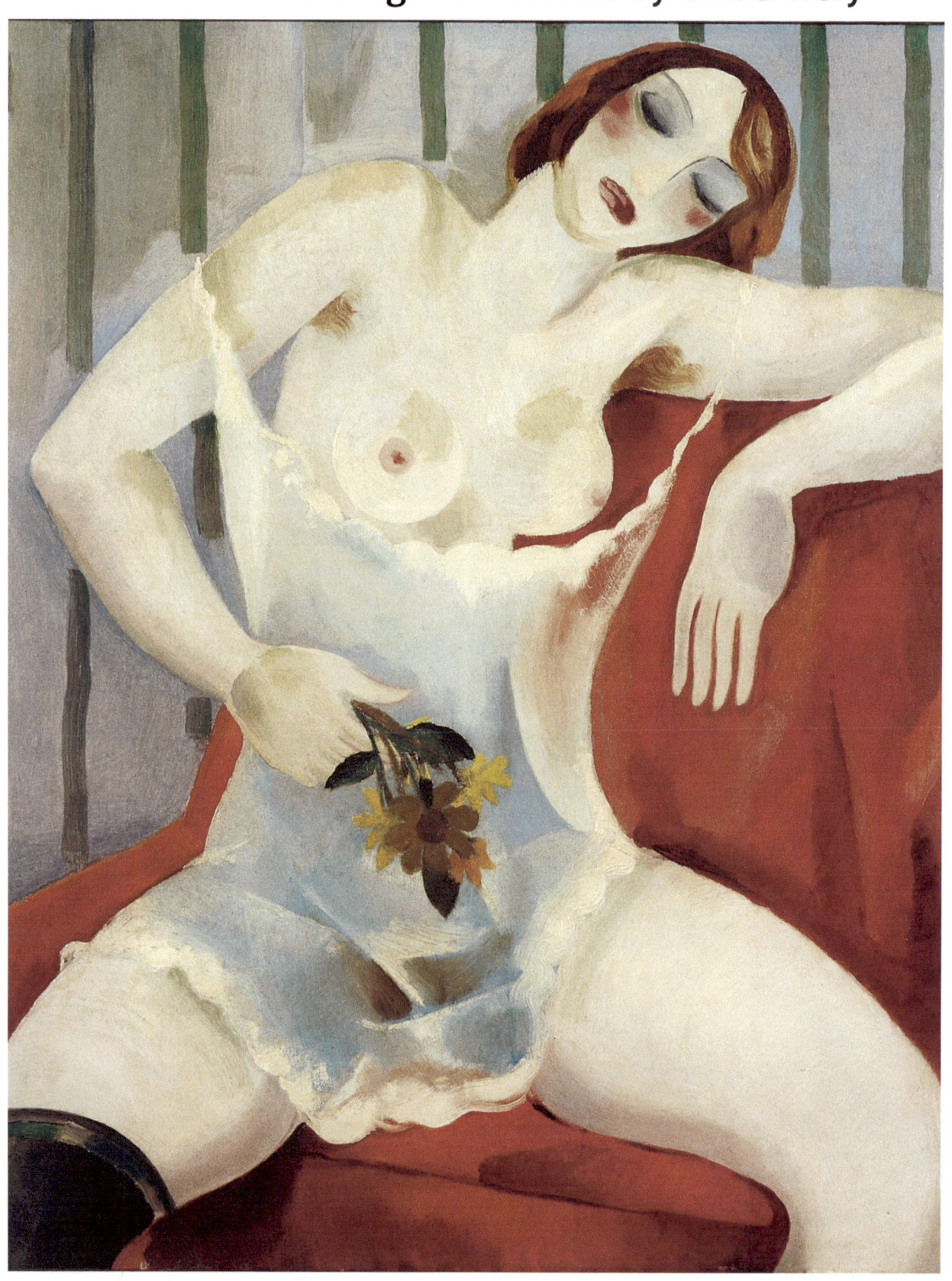

Nude Woman with Arm Across Forehead by Felix Vollotton

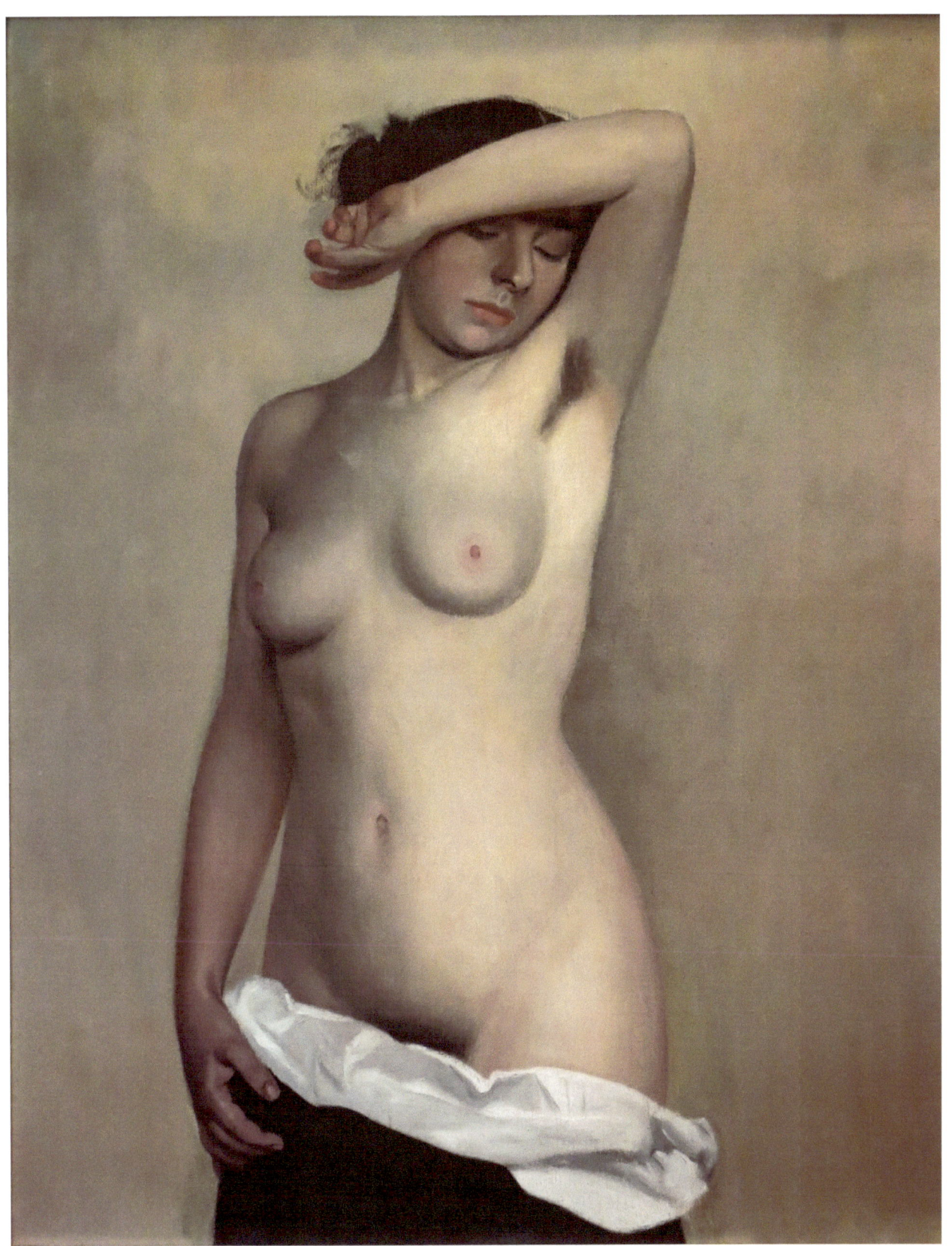

Nude From Behind by William Merritt Chase

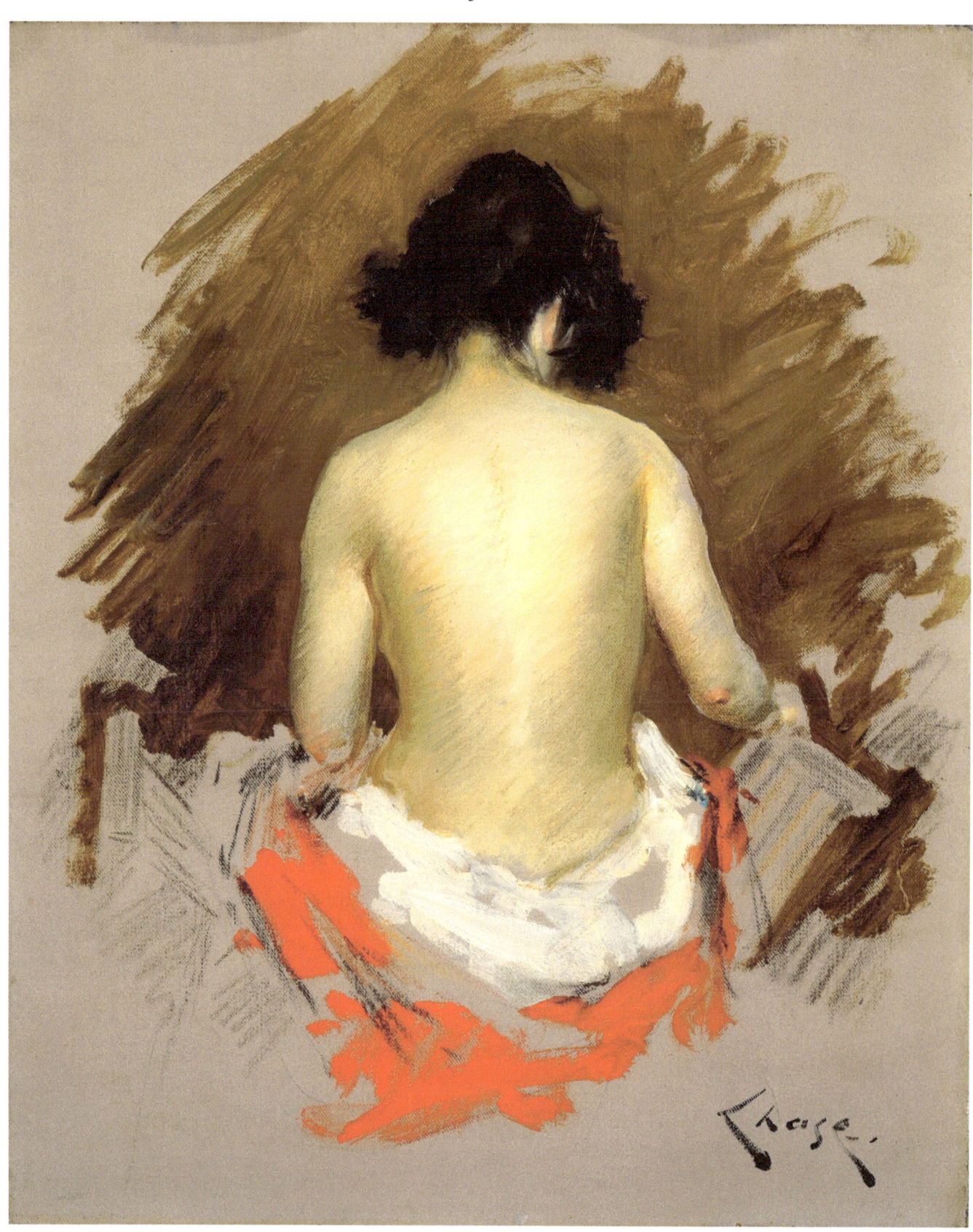

About the Author

Carl Scott Harker resides in a small coastal town in Southern Oregon. When he his not writing and editing books, he runs a small photography business.

Other Books by the Author Available on Amazon

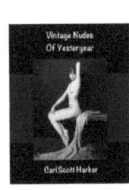 **"Vintage Nudes of Yesteryear"** presents sixty-five black and white photos of nude women produced generally between the years 1900 and 1923. It can be found on Amazon here: https://www.amazon.com/Vintage-Nudes-Yesteryear-Scott-Harker/dp/107044023X.

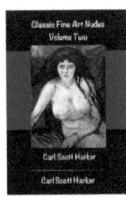 **"Classic Fine Art Nudes: Volume Two."** This book is the second book in a series collecting classic fine art nudes and is available on Amazon at https://www.amazon.com/Classic-Fine-Art-Nudes-Two/dp/1711917583.

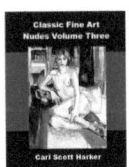 **"Classic Fine Art Nudes: Volume Three."** This book is the third book in a series collecting classic fine art nudes and is available on Amazon at https://amzn.to/3mAAK1N.

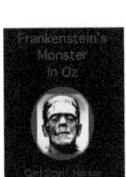 **"Frankenstein's Monster in Oz"** This book tells the story of how Frankenstein's Monster comes to Oz and what happens to him there. It is available on Amazon at https://www.amazon.com/Frankensteins-Monster-Carl-Scott-Harker/dp/1707291365.

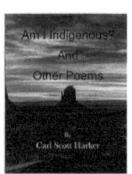 **"Am I Indigenous and Other Poems"** – A collection of poems written between late 2016 and Autumn 2019. This book can be found on Amazon here: https://www.amazon.com/Am-I-Indigenous-Other-Poems/dp/1689862424.

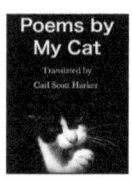 **"Poems By My Cat"** – These poems reveal how cats view the world. The book can be found on Amazon here: https://www.amazon.com/Poems-Cat-Carl-Scott-Harker/dp/1793903239.

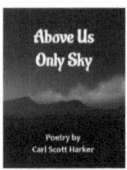 **"Above Us Only Sky"** – This book of poetry features poems written between late April, 2020 to late October, 2020. You will find this book here: https://amzn.to/38kb83R.

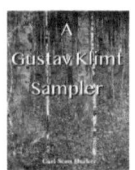 **"A Gustav Klimt Sampler "** – Here is a collection of 46 paintings and drawings by the Austrian artist Gustav Klimt. This is a sampling of his best work. The book is available on Amazon at https://www.amazon.com/Gustav-Klimt-Sampler-Great-Artists-ebook/dp/B084V1W3L7.

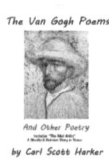 **"The Van Gogh Poems and Other Poetry"** - This book features a collection of poems written in late 2019 and early 2020. The first 17 poems were inspired by paintings by Vincent Van Gogh. The book is available on Amazon at https://amzn.to/38Hq6Tg.

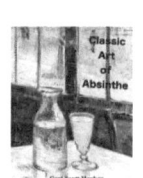 **"Classic Art of Absinthe"** - This book collects the best of the classic artwork about absinthe from the makers of absinthe, those who wanted absinthe banned and the artists of the time (mid-1800's to early 1900's). It is available on Amazon at https://www.amazon.com/Classic-Absinthe-Carl-Scott-Harker/dp/1653501189.

www.ingramcontent.com/pod-product-compliance
Lightning Source LLC
Chambersburg PA
CBHW041315180526

45172CB00004B/1112